You Have A
DAM
Problem

**How to Identify and Change the Behaviors
Sabotaging Your Company**

You Have A
DAM
Problem

How to Identify and Change the Behaviors
Sabotaging Your Company

GRAY MCQUARRIE

▤BOUND
▢PUBLISHING

Bound Publishing
A division of Dean Global Group Inc.

United States
6501 E. Greenway Pkwy
#103-480
Scottsdale, AZ
85254

Canada
Suite 114
720 28th St. NE
Calgary, AB T2A 6R3

Toll Free Phone and Fax: 1-888-237-1627
Email: info@boundpublishing.com

ISBN (softcover):   978-0-9867762-9-8
ISBN (ebook):   978-0-9881235-3-3

Cover: Kamal Singh
Text: Gray McQuarrie
Edit: Bound Publishing

ACKNOWLEDGEMENTS

I would like to thank George Parachou and Bill Brandell for reading multiple versions of this book over the last couple of years. The hours of questions and discussions proved to be invaluable. And George was always there as a sounding board as well as a bit of a whip in order to get me to the finish line and complete this book. I would like to thank Todd Dean for encouraging me to even start this second book, when I was reluctant to at first. His honest criticism was invaluable to me, as well as getting others to read earlier versions of the book and get their input. I would like to thank those who read individual chapters and provided their insights to me both good and bad, like Anita Allen who is the Anita in the chapter concerning the demise of my Jeep sinking in the Verdi River in Arizona. And to Carl Schott, who is the Colonel I talk about in the Epilogue. For everyone who worked with me on this project I would not have persisted in it without everyone's encouragement.

I would like to thank Dr. Edward Humphrey who was a very close friend and life long working partner of my father. They were a team and what they built together at the Minneapolis VAMC, with the combined Thoracic Surgery program with a research medical Ph.D. was a great contribution to medicine and surgery. When Dr. Humphrey hired me to work in the research laboratories during the summers while I attended St. Olaf, I learned how humiliating the scientific method could be on the huge egos of very smart MDs. They quickly learned their righteous opinions were often wrong. And with their realization I witnessed ego DAMs being crushed for the first time. Through Dr. Humphrey's example of how he led his team's ups and downs I learned the absolute strength of humility. And the MDs that chose to take up the challenge of the program quickly learned that Dr. Humphrey might appear to be slow, but within a few weeks they were quickly scrambling to keep up with him. And after several months they had a combination of fear and awe for the man: fear that they had better be prepared for each meeting and awe that he was going to add a new twist, insight, or research publication that got them around what appeared to be an impossible roadblock.

CONTENTS

CONTENTS

FOREWORD

The Attractive Power of Stories

If you lived today as if it were your last, you'd buy up a box of rockets and fire them all off, wouldn't you?

—Garrison Keillor

Very rarely do I go to Catholic mass. I remember one day going to a large Catholic church in downtown Phoenix that had a large Hispanic following. There was a strong sense of community, family, and friends. You saw it, sensed it. Even though I really don't like going to church, I was already feeling at home, even though my mind was telling me I would be much happier being somewhere else and doing something else.

The priest was young and as he started his sermon, he didn't seem rehearsed. He didn't seem to know what he wanted to say. His apparent discomfort made me uncomfortable, and even though I didn't want to listen, I couldn't stop listening. I was trying to figure out where he was going; then I could tune him out. He started to tell a story about how a man kept on apologizing for being Catholic. Being raised Catholic myself, this is a very easy thing to do. We always seem to be apologizing. The message that was emerging from his awkward telling of his story was it was OK to be Catholic. In fact, "In this parish we should all make t-shirts that say, 'Catholic Pride.'" We all laughed. Catholic pride was an oxymoron! And what I was listening to and looking at was something truly remarkable; a Catholic priest that was an iconoclast! Somehow this totally imperfect priest saying these really imperfect almost blasphemous things, had me very attracted. I wanted to come back and listen again. How was he able to convince me to do what I absolutely didn't want to do with such simple words, simple language, and simple ideas told in such an imperfect, but very human way? What is it about a story told like this that attracts us? What is it about a story told like this that connects us?

It's this power to attract that forms the engine of the universe. An astronaut on a shuttle mission mixed some dirt, some sugar, and some water in a bag and observed what happened. The dust in the water in the weightlessness of space started to clump together. More sophisticated experiments have been conducted again and again. They all come back with the same thing. Dust clumps together in the weightlessness of space. And this growth happens exponentially. It supports the Planetismal Theory: Planets are formed initially from cosmic dust.

The dust on this book that seems so insignificant to you has the ability to attract other dust in the right environment, which will eventually create a planet. How big does this dust ball have to get before gravity starts to kick in? According to the theory, just one kilometer in diameter. At that point things really start to get interesting and you get moon size balls called protoplanets. Can we see this happening in the universe? Actually we can. The *Spire* within M16 of the Eagle Nebula is awe inspiring. After seeing this image, you will never look at a dust ball in the same way ever again. Great big things can be created from a bunch of little things. You just need the right environment.

One summer my dad used to drive me to work on his way to work. We would listen to a small local morning radio show called the Prairie Home Companion. It was basically Garrison Keillor talking about things and telling stories, like stories about his cat, for two hours. I would initially think what I was listening to was stupid. But, I couldn't stop listening. I would chuckle and then laugh and so would my dad. Garrison's story attracted our attention. And by enjoying his stories, my dad and I felt connected.

Hardly anyone knew of the show at first, but more and more people started listening to it on their radio. As his morning show grew listeners, Keillor decided to start a variety show on the weekends. There wasn't much risk and the station needed its air time filled, so they let him do it. The first variety show was done on July 6th, 1974 at the Janet Wallace Auditorium at Macalester College in Minneapolis, Minnesota. Twelve people showed up for the audience. Today, his show, where its home is the Fitzgerald Theater, in St. Paul, Minnesota, travels all around the world and is broadcast to millions of listeners. It is one of the most significant shows National Public Radio has ever had. And it just started with one person and one microphone telling stories about his cats in the morning. It started like a particle of dust collecting other particles of dust, becoming more and more significant until all sorts of interesting and talented people were attracted, creating something very special for all of us to listen to if we chose. For me, his show has become my church. It nourishes my soul and reminds me of my dad.

Too many companies look at what people accomplish, where they went to school, how confident they are in what they say, and whether they have ever made any mistakes. Interviews are just a simple question and answer format where people deciding to hire have already made up their mind based on first impressions. This process of hiring people has proven again and again to be wrong. The legacy of American business these days is not a good one and the people that are attracted and hired to the top jobs seem to be criminals. Why is this? It's because we are looking at the wrong things and doing it the wrong way. We fail to look for the most obvious character we need to build a top-notch company: The ability of the leader to attract top-notch talent.

What we need to ask a future leader of our business is, "Do you have the power to attract talent?" Then you have to demand, "Prove it to me by telling me your story." And then we need to listen to their story very carefully. If you aren't attracted, you are likely not talking to the right candidate. If it is too perfect, you are likely not talking to the right candidate. If it doesn't appeal to your humanity, you are likely not talking to the right candidate.

A great leader of a great business simply creates the right environment to attract others where growth is a consequence. When you have the right leadership and the right talent more talent will naturally be attracted and just like the dust in the Eagle Nebula in the weightlessness of space, a miracle will happen: Your company will grow on its own to become a brilliant star.

If this isn't happening in your company right now and in this moment *You Have a DAM Problem!*

—Gray McQuarrie
July, 2012

PROLOGUE

A Lasting Legacy of Heart

You know you've got to stop going around this hospital and telling patients you're Dr. Wangensteen!

—A young intern named Norm Shumway to Dr. Owen Wagensteen in front of patients on an early morning surgery round.

The University of Minnesota Surgical Alumnus list reads like a who's who of thoracic, open heart, and transplant surgeons. I know of all the awards my dad received there was no greater honor for him then to be on this list. I have highlighted the great men I knew when I grew up and describe a little about them.

UNIVERSITY OF MINNESOTA
SURGICAL ALUMNUS OF THE YEAR

1978—Dr. Owen H. Wangensteen

1979—Dr. Lloyd D. MacLean

1980—Dr. Norman E. Shumway

1981—Dr. K. Alvin Merendino

1982—Dr. Richard L. Varco

1983—Dr. Gilbert S. Campbell

1984—Dr. Ward O. Griffen, Jr.

1985—Dr. Stanley R. Friesen

1986—Dr. Clarence Dennis

1987—Dr. F. John Lewis

1988—Dr. C. Walton Lillehei

1989—Dr. Aldo R. Castaeda

1990—Dr. J. Bradley Aust

1991—Dr. Mitchell W. Spellman

1992—Dr. Vincent L. Gott

1993—Dr. Morley Cohen

1994—Dr. Donald J. Ferguson

1995—Dr. Lyle A. French

1996—Dr. Ronald M. Ferguson

1997—Dr. Edward W. Humphrey

1998—Dr. Wallace P. Ritchie, Jr.

1999—Dr. Donald G. McQuarrie

DR. OWEN H. WANGENSTEEN

Served as chairman of the University of Minnesota's Surgery Department from 1930 until 1967. Fondly called "The Chief." In 1930 he was appointed as the first head for the U of M's department of surgery. He started with one surgery fellow and two interns.

He was exceptionally skilled at identifying and attracting the best talent in the field. Dr. Christiaan Barnard studied under him and took away much of Dr. Norman Shumway's work, to do the first heart transplant in South Africa. The worlds first successful open heart surgery was performed in 1952. F. John Lewis, assisted by Richard L. Varco, and C. Walton Lillehei closed an arterial secundum defect in a 5 year old girl under direct vision, using inflow stasis and moderate total-body hypothermia. If this sounds on the cutting edge of its day...well it was way over the edge and into the unheard of. This was the kind of talent and innovation Wangensteen attracted by the environment and culture he nurtured within the surgery department. It has been generally accepted that Owen's department of surgery was the most innovative and the very best in the world during his tenure.

When he retired in 1967, he presided over 100 surgical fellows, 18 interns, and 200 surgical beds.

My dad, as a young man, had a somewhat bitter relationship with Owen, because he rejected my dad's desire to work side by side with Richard L. Varco, which at the time was the most prestigious position one could have. Later, I think my dad realized that this rejection was the greatest thing that could have ever happened to him. Owen came to many of my parent's parties and I could see my dad's love for him. I found him to be a very tall, curious man who gave me his complete attention when I was in his presence. Owen seemed to know what was best for my dad, because my dad and

Dr. Humphrey created one of the finest thoracic surgery programs in the world at the Minneapolis Veteran's Administration Hospital.

A landmark high rise building on the University of Minnesota campus is the Phillips-Wangensteen building in the Academic Health Sciences complex. He was tireless in his pursuit of funds to create this building and a base for a world-class historical library and degree program in the history of medicine. In order to have the funds to make this building and center possible, he did two things. First, he set a limit on the amount of personal income he would accept from his own practice and turned over any excess to a University Surgical Research Fund. Secondly, he wrote his more affluent private patients a letter saying he preferred not to bill them, requesting instead that they send a contribution to the Fund in an amount they themselves deemed appropriate.

Owen's success was not defined by his singular individual accomplishment, but by his ability to attract the very best talent in the world and have them work as a team.

Dr. Norman E. Shumway

Trained under Owen H. Wangensteen, Shumway left the U of M in 1958 to go to Stanford. where he built one of the world's most distinguished cardiovascular departments. Even though he was the first surgeon to perform a heart transplant in the United States, the actual procedure didn't have a high success rate and was abandoned by everyone, except Shumway. Shumway persevered. He and his team at Stanford took on the monumental task of working out every single detail required to make heart transplantation a safe and routine procedure. This took several decades of work. One of the great breakthroughs was the development and use of an immunosuppressive drug.

When you attract great talent you can't predict what the talent will do. This is the hallmark of a Maverick. When Owen called Shumway into his office one day, disgusted that he had only produced seven publications when he expected several dozen, Norm said, "Well, you could actually read [my] publications."

Despite the tensions, Shumway very much appreciated Wagensteen. *[Owen's] job was to be sure that the troops had enough support. It was a remarkable attitude, particularly for those days.*

I grew up thinking Norman Shumway was the Greek god Thor, because of the many stories my dad would tell about the man. His sense of humor and his iconoclastic and maverick ways were legendary. I wasn't there, but one time long after Shumway retired from Stanford he joined my father, mom, and sister to play golf at a country club in Minnesota. He got there early and took a golf cart, but didn't bother to go all the way to the driving range. Stopping at the chipping green, adjacent to the range, was much more convenient for him. He gathered up some balls, teed them up on the green, and proceeded to hit drives going perpendicular to the range where some shots were angling towards the golfers on the range. When my sister was sent to go fetch Shumway, she was shocked. She went down and very politely explained that it was time to go to the first hole. Shumway saw nothing wrong with his creative use of the chipping green area to work on his drives.

Shumway's daughter, Sara J. Shumway, is the Vice Chief, Division of Cardiothoracic Surgery at the University of Minnesota. She has also served as the surgical director of heart transplantation and is the current surgical director of lung transplantation.

Dr. Richard L. Varco

Dr. Varco was one of the pioneers of open heart surgery. He joined the department of surgery faculty under Owen Wagensteen in 1943. Besides being part of the team to perform the first open heart surgery, he was also part of the team that performed the first open-heart operation using cross-circulation. He led the first jejunoileal bypass operations in 1953. He started the transplant program at the Univeristy of Minnesota where he performed a kidney transplant between two identical twin sisters. He was also credited by Dr. John Najarian in 2002: "Varco's influence was also responsible for keeping and training the key principle investigators and clinicians in heart transplantation, including Christiaan A. Barnard and Norman E. Shumway, the world pioneers in this field."

Varco was legendary for his tough exterior. In Wayne Miller's book about Dr. Lillehei, entitled "King of Hearts," he describes Varco as "a demanding, sometimes gruff man who scared the more timid younger residents. Short and beefy, with a shot of thick black hair, had big paws for hands—meeting him on the street you might have guessed he worked the waterfront. But in fact, he was the slickest of the University of Minnesota surgeons, and that included the Chief."

My mom went to the University of Minnesota in the 1950s to study nursing. The program was intense, and one year she had to spend time learning how to be a surgery nurse under Varco. One day, there appeared a dashing young surgery resident who had been assigned to be broken in by Varco. Varco had never met him and was rude and gruff to him, and did his best to make this young man nervous. Nothing seemed to work. During the course of the operation, the young man accidentally stabbed Varco's hand with a knife. Varco lambasted him. But the young man wasn't fazed. He simply looked Varco straight in the eyes and said, "My apologies Dr. Varco. I am just a simple country boy trying to make it in the big time." The whole room laughed, including Varco. The young surgeon was my dad. He courted my mom relentlessly. And Richard Varco became a close family friend whom I always saw him as a type of Santa Claus. He always seemed to be happy around my mom and my dad.

Dr. C. Walton Lillehei

Walt Lillehei was world-renowned and his name still carries great reverence and remains legendary in the field of thoracic surgery. In 1958, assisted by Varco, he led the team on an open-heart surgery using cross circulation, and a device that Earl Bakken, co-counder of Medtronic had designed, the world's first portable, battery-operated pacemaker. Lillehei developed and implanted the world's first prosthetic heart valves, the Lillehei-Nakib toroidal disk, the Lillehei-Kaster pivoting disk, and the Kalke-Lillehei rigid bileaflet prosthesis. For many at the department, Lillehei was considered to be the most intellectually talented of this unbelievable team Owen had assembled.

I can't recall meeting Walton. But when my dad talked about him it was with supreme admiration.

Dr. Donald G. McQuarrie

Here is what was said after my dad's passing.

"After completing his surgical internship and residency at the University of Minnesota and serving in the navy, Dr. McQuarrie became a thoracic surgeon for the Minneapolis Veterans Administration Medical Center, where he eventually became Chief of Surgery. Dr. McQuarrie was a member of the University of Minnesota's surgical faculty for more than 37 years. He also chaired numerous medical organizations and committees, held a number of visiting professorships, and authored medical textbooks. In 1999, the Minnesota Surgical Residents Society named him Surgical Alumnus of the year."

My dad loved every minute of every day being part of this medical community with a rich heritage and a proud tradition.

I know my dad is with these great men today—Wangensteen, Shumway, Varco, Lillehei, and the others. When my mom and my dad were dating, working in the University of Minnesota medical center, she would be invited around dinnertime to sit at the big round table with my dad and these great men. My mom was extremely smart and extremely strong willed. To say my dad had his hands full was an understatement. She was the only female granted as a guest at this table. All of these great medical pioneers would eat, smoke, drink, and discuss topics of history, philosophy, literature, politics, farming, art, theater, religion, science (not medical), and astronomy, going on for hours. When my mom speaks of this time I can tell it was one of the happiest times my mom and my dad spent together. A time that looked from afar to be so ordinary and natural, but in actual fact was extraordinary and very ephemeral. She treasures those memories as if they were a valued diamond in her jewel box, realizing that such a meeting of minds would never emerge in this way again. The product and contribution that was made to medicine by these great unselfish men will remain a long lasting legacy for the world to enjoy. What they did represents the very best humanity can be.

This book is dedicated to my late father,
Dr. Donald Gray McQuarrie, M.D., Ph.D.

A DAM REVIEW

Work is Social

For those of you who didn't read my first book, *Change Your DAM Thinking*, let me take you on a quick DAM review so you don't get lost in this book. In my first book I made the claim that 1) work is social; 2) behaviors lead results; and 3) our behaviors are governed by our thinking.

Despite what you might have read in some complicated book about business life cycles, there are really only four business states as shown in Table 1.

Table 1: The Four Business States

	Paradigm	
	DAM Thinking	**FLOW Thinking**
Reality	Dysfunction	Unlimited Growth
Fantasy	Disaster	Goal Seeking

Unlimited Growth is the preferred state where you operate within the Flow Thinking Paradigm and deal with the Reality of running your business. Unfortunately, nothing stays the same. The world flows and you have to either anticipate change—Goal Seeking; adapt to the change—Dysfunction; or ignore the change—Disaster. If you avoid the Goal Seeking quadrant, because you don't want to cannibalize and wreck what your company is doing today, you could quickly be gone tomorrow. This simple construct explains any business life cycle, a life cycle led by our behavior, which is governed by our thinking.

So what is FLOW thinking? It's two things. It is the absence of DAM thinking and it is having six characteristics embedded in your company culture. We call these characteristics the six musts for FLOW. These musts are 1) skill; 2) standards; 3) commitment; 4) accountability; 5) observation; and 6) improvisation.

The Thinking DAMs are described in Table 2.

Table 2: The Five Thinking DAMs

The _____ Dam Stops	The Flow of _____
Ego	Productivity
Feelings	Purpose
Trust	Communication
My Precious	Territory (Growth)
Learning	Discovery

These DAMs are meant to be understood in a few minutes. When you don't ask for help, because of your pride and unwillingness to show weakness, problems grow. This is the Ego DAM and it blocks productivity. If you choose to manage people's feelings, and say it is OK to be late with an order, you have made your employee's feelings more important than the company. This is the Feelings DAM and it blocks purpose. If you are out to get my job and make me look bad, then we will not communicate freely and openly. This is the Trust DAM that blocks communication. If you won't let anyone know anything about your job, or won't let them be involved in your invention, or won't help them do the same work you do, you will be forever stuck and so will your company. This is the My Precious DAM and it blocks territory and growth. Finally if you think you know everything—you are a know it all—then you will never discover anything new. You will have a Learning DAM and this blocks discovery. In the DAM thinking paradigm, work is not social. In FLOW thinking, work is social. FLOW thinking is about productivity, purpose, communication, territory, and discovery. DAM thinking is a stagnant, polluted void of innovation and creativity.

You know you are operating in a DAM thinking paradigm when you experience pressure, stagnation, and pollution. You know you are operating in a FLOW thinking paradigm when you experience velocity, quality, and emergence.

ABOUT THIS BOOK

It became clear after writing the first book, *Change Your DAM Thinking*, that I had to write this second book. The first reason was too many people told me they loved the book because they could see the DAM problem in others. These same people, of course, didn't see a DAM problem in themselves. That is why the end of each chapter has questions you must answer, along with an honest friend (someone who won't buy into your Feelings DAM baggage), so you can truly discover if you, yourself, have a DAM problem.

The second reason I wrote this book was because I got a number of questions concerning which DAM is the worst or which DAM needs to be worked on first. Really, it doesn't matter where you start. Fixing one DAM starts to fix them all. Be that as it may, this question got me thinking about how the DAMs stack and what happens. Figure 1 shows how the Thinking DAMS stack.

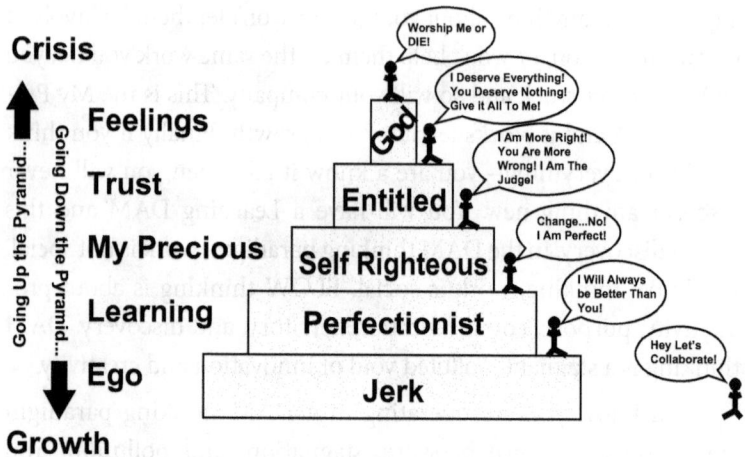

Figure 1:
The pyramid of separation.

The construct in Figure 1 helps us recognize, more precisely, which DAMs are operating in ourselves as well as in others. For example, if you ask an honest friend, would they typically say you are a jerk? If so, then there is a strong likelihood you have an Ego DAM. If you have a Learning DAM, you likely have an Ego DAM too, and this means you want everything in your world to be perfect. Because the DAMs stack, if you are a Perfectionist you are also a Jerk. This stacking of the first two DAMs should be pretty easy for you to see.

You might wonder, right off the bat, why the Feelings DAM is stacked at the top. Couldn't you have a Feelings DAM only? Not usually. Think of a child who throws a tantrum because he isn't getting his own way. Is he able to move into new territory? No. That is why the space at the top of the DAM pyramid in Figure 1 is so small. We are at our worst when we have lost all emotional control. Our one and only thought is of self. At that point we have become a person with a God complex who is an entitled, self-righteous, perfectionistic jerk.

Be that as it may, it is fairly common to have only a feelings DAM. This usually happens when a manager is confronted with a God complex or what I call in Chapter 5 a Rock Star employee, where they put the purpose of the company second to making the seemingly indespensible Rock Star happy. This never works out well.

After the Introduction where I talk about my dad and the way he died, we enter Part 1 of the book. We climb the pyramid. Think of an ancient Egyptian pyramid, or a mountain, or some Inca temple. Since the dawn of civilization, we have desired to be higher, holier, or better than others. I don't know about you, but when I am up high I say, "Ok the view is great, but if I am going to get anything done it is time to get down off this thing." We climb from Jerk, to Perfectinist, to Righteous, to Entitled, to Rock Star within the first five chapters.

Now the Rock Star isn't alone on top of his pyramid. He is accompanied by a victim; a victim that is willing to sacrifice her life to keep the Rock Star happy! Not only that the Rock Star himself is also a victim too. It's complicated up there. Chapter 6 is about the victim and the complicated relationship with the Rock Star.

Starting in Chapter 8, we work our way down off this pyramid. We talk about firing your Rock Star (probably the scariest thing you will ever have to do), being grateful for what you have and that understanding God's Protection is Rejection in Chapter 9, be Iconoclast or hire an Iconoclast in Chapter 10, declare you are Incompetent in Chapter 11, and Don't Shoot the Messenger in Chapter 12.

I didn't mention Chapter 7 did I? You are probably wondering where you find the solution to your problems and how you become a FLOW thinker. Well you needn't go far, because the solution is within your four walls. Don't expect me to coddle you or spoon feed you answers. You must think! Pay attention to what I say about coming to grips with your Rock Star. Stop complaining and be grateful for what you have now. Yes it is that easy and that hard.

I end with the epilogue. I really, truly love a great forward and introduction and a great epilogue to any book I read. They are like wonderful book ends. I hope you are entertained, that you learn something, and that this book improves your world of business by making it a bit more understandable and you a better person. We can always be better people.

INTRODUCTION

Ultimately, we're all dead men!

Ultimately, we're all dead men. Sadly we cannot choose how, but what we can decide is how we meet that end in order that we are remembered, as men.

—Proximo from the movie *Gladiator* (2000)

The morning light filled the bedroom of my parent's home. The early spring day wanted to be cheerful, but it was impossible. My mom held my dad's hand. My dad was dying. These were the last hours of his life. He struggled to breathe. I noticed his lips moving. He was saying something over and over again. I couldn't make it out so I put my ear very close. He was saying, "I love you all. I love you all. I love you all." He kept on repeating this as his eyes closed. Shortly after, my dad died peacefully. He was 76.

Many people attended my dad's remembrance. However if my dad would have had his way, there would have been no remembrance.

He didn't want to bother people and disrupt their lives with sadness. He didn't think much of sentimentality. He always wanted to be actively moving forward. He did this by traveling, jewelry-making, cooking, learning, lecturing, teaching, writing, reading, listening to music, thinking, joking, and observing.

Spending time with people always turned into an event when my father was involved. His people-time had to be intelligent. It had to be fun. It had to be surprising. It was never boring. My dad's ego could fill an airplane hangar. And people loved him for it. He was confident, well-spoken, and jovial. You knew where he was from a mile away. There is nothing wrong with a big confident ego and my dad was proof of that.

My dad loved eccentric people who had that special glimmer of intelligence he could see in their eyes. One of my dad's sayings was, "The difference between being eccentric and crazy is money." He knew if he saw that eccentric glint in a person's eyes, that person would love a good story. My dad loved a good story. To him, a story was the greatest gift you could give someone else. If you weren't going to tell one, he would. But, if you were telling a good one, he would be very quiet and listen for every detail, every subtlety, how you told it, and the words you used; likely because he not only wanted to understand it, he also wanted to retell it.

Dad looked for the flaws in the characters of the story, as well as the character you were playing by telling the story. He knew it was the flaws that added the color. He knew something perfect would be robotic and stripped of meaning. A screwed up fact, something you forgot and went back and retold, a quirky thing you did—he watched for all of this. And he would never, ever interrupt your story. He knew all stories had a rhythm. He knew the spaces between the words and paragraphs were part of the meaning. The intonations, the hand gestures; he saw all of these as important parts of your performance. He absorbed it all. And he would be thoroughly entertained by your gift of sharing something important about yourself. If you told a really good story, he would reward you with a long pause. And then he would offer a few words that would give you an insight you never considered before.

At the remembrance service, each of us in the room remembered my father by telling stories to each other. But everyone knew the greatest story teller was gone, forever. I could feel the void, a void I knew I could never fill. Dr. J.T. Lee, who worked closely with my father, pulled me aside. "Listen to me, Gray," he said. "Your dad will always be there. He will never leave you." He repeated it to me again, "Gray, he will never leave you."

At the time I didn't know what he meant by that but, as I write this book, I know he is with me now. J. T. was right. It's easy to be angry at a parent for dying. I felt he was too young. We all did. It wasn't fair! It was easy to feel angry and hurt. It was easy to feel entitled to more. It was easy to feel completely lost. But, *God's protection is rejection.* A loss brings people together. Help is all around you if you are willing to drop your guard, drop your Ego DAM. I didn't ask for J.T.'s help. I pretended I didn't need it. And I let it in anyway because I did need it. J.T. was right. My dad will never leave me.

My dad was a thoracic surgeon at the Minneapolis Veteran's Administration Medical Center. He was Director of the Surgical Research Laboratory, Professor of Surgery at the University of Minnesota, and eventually became Chief of Surgery at the Minneapolis VAMC. He wrote two great textbooks on surgery. He was truly talented and gifted at what he did in the operating room. More than that, he was gifted at finding just the talent he needed to have a great surgical team. He wanted to have his team focused and alert but also relaxed, flexible, and able to respond with its best to any emergency. As a leader, he knew that if he used fear and intimidation with his team, the patient would likely end up dead. He learned to acknowledge the members of his team for what they did well, and to offer them positive reinforcement. From time to time, he would need to articulate the standards he expected them to uphold; but he never did that during an operation. He knew surgery was a time to be flexible. Sometimes he would lead and other times the team would lead. It was a give-and-take orchestration of precision that was unpredictable and the agenda was set by circumstances which were real and immediate. Operations could last many hours and the team had to stay sharp. During the boring parts of a procedure he kept his team's mental acuity up by telling stories.

My dad never complained about his surgery teams or gave any hint that a team had ever let him down. He knew how to hire people, which is a skill few managers in business possess. I think he was successful because he always looked for the character of the person and knew he could uncover that character if the person shared a story with him. My dad always talked about his teams with great reverence and supreme respect, often telling me stories about the people on them. This made me curious about what it was like to work with him in the operating room.

I had a glimpse of this when he worked on his jewelry in our house. My dad would be at his workbench and I would go back and forth, in and out, opening and closing doors, as would my mom, my sister, or a repairman. But my dad, who worked carefully on his jewelry with a set of precision tools (holding them as a surgeon holds a scalpel), carved patiently and precisely, and would not be interrupted. He was completely in the moment, in his own zone. The only way I could interrupt him was to walk up and say, "Dad, I don't get this math problem." He would look up, his eyes ten sizes larger because of the magnification helmet he wore, with a surprised, happy smile and say, "Show it to me." We would work on it together and then he would go back to his jewelry-making. He could work like that for hours.

I heard stories about my dad in the operating room, when he stood uninterrupted for hours, highly focused, working delicately with his hands while he guided his team and they helped and guided him. It was a superhuman demonstration of concentration, delicate precision, supreme endurance, and strength that sometimes lasted the better part of a day and he could repeat it for days on end.

It's easy to think of great surgeons like my father as gods—people who are different from you and me. And in a way they are, even as they are also very human. My dad was able to push himself beyond his limits and keep going. But it cost him; his knees, back, and hands eventually failed him. He kept much of the physical pain to himself. He was too proud to say he was less than what he appeared. Doctors make bad patients and my dad was no exception. He didn't ask for help. None of us knew what he was keeping from us. My dad had an Ego DAM.

It was a very understandable Ego DAM. It wasn't just about whether he admitted he had problems, it was also how he protected his family. Rightly or wrongly, he kept many of his weaknesses to himself. It was what defined him and there was no changing it. He was never going to compromise his principles. It is very difficult to argue that keeping his health issues to himself was the wrong thing.

My dad grew up in the small town of Richfield in central Utah, where his dad, John Gray McQuarrie, was a family doctor with a territory that covered hundreds of square miles. My dad would often travel with him. When there was a distant medical emergency, my father and grandfather often reached their destination on horseback.

Sometimes my grandfather would have to operate, on the spot, with my father assisting. In this way my dad learned medicine long before his first day of medical school and he dreamed of becoming a great surgeon.

My dad feared he would be stuck in Richfield. He hated working in the fields during the summer, digging and building fences. He dreamed of a life outside of Richfield and this drove him to excel. He practiced the piano for hours, eventually attaining the skill of a concert pianist. He read every book in the massive Carnegie-endowed public library down the road. His love for writing grew. He began to see himself as an author of fiction who would contribute to the world of literature, like a modern day F. Scott Fitzgerald or Hemingway.

This intellectual growth was a mixed blessing. He wanted to be a great surgeon because of the work he did with his father. He wanted to be a great author because of his enormous capacity to remember stories he read, many of which supercharged his imagination. This created a conflict in his life that was never wholly resolved.

At the University of Utah he was offered a Rhodes Scholarship. This scholarship program, set up by Cecil Rhodes in 1902 and still in force today, allows the most creative, gifted, and intellectually talented young people from around the world to go to Oxford University in England to study anything they choose. It is considered the world's most prestigious scholarship. People who attain it almost always go on to be the top experts in their fields.

My dad wanted to go to Oxford and immerse himself in literature and think about the great book he would write; a book that would capture people's imagination. Then, he could return to the study of medicine. This dream did not sit well with my grandfather, who didn't understand it. He thought a career in medicine would be better and believed if my dad went to Oxford he would never become a doctor. This was despite my dad's hope of juggling two careers as an English professor and an M.D. My dad chose to follow his father's wishes. It was a decision that haunted him for the rest of his life. Many people at his remembrance were glad he didn't go to Oxford. If he had, none of us would have known him. I wouldn't be writing to you now.

The dream remained present in his heart. On his desk was a tattered, unabridged Oxford dictionary, something you would not expect to see on a surgeon's desk. It was where he turned to find the perfect word for a letter, memo, lecture, article or book he was writing. If you looked through his library, studied where he traveled, and observed what he collected, you would know that in his heart, my dad wanted to be an author. And though he wrote two distinguished textbooks, he devoted his life to surgery.

I learned a lot from my dad about people and business. One summer, when I was about seven, we went to the Green Giant canning plant in Glencoe, Minnesota. I remember him being very happy. He didn't talk much while he drove, but he was excited to show this operation to me. He knew it would leave an impression.

I remember the scene like it was yesterday. My dad parked next to a sunken conveyor belt, where trucks dumped great piles of corn and bulldozers pushed the corn stalks in. It was well coordinated, a fast-moving dance. Everyone looked focused and many had smiles on their faces. They loved their work.

In the distant fields you could see the combines cut corn and people went in and out of the canning building. Everything was moving; dust was everywhere; nothing stopped.

Apparently, each corn pile had been graded. Codes were shouted out as the type of seed was noted. Dad helped me hold a large burlap bag that was much taller than me, as it was filled with corn. We filled two of these bags and took them home. My sister and I used a wheelbarrow to enthusiastically haul one of the bags from house to house. We knocked on the doors and asked, "Do you want some corn?" "No, we aren't interested kids," our neighbors would reply. But we were persistent, "It's really good. You really should try some. Just take a few ears. They're free." So they took a few ears, closed the doors and hoped it was enough to make us go away. We got back home with the bag still half full.

About a week later, some neighbors came and asked for more free corn. Fresh Green Giant corn was the best-tasting corn on the planet. Seriously, it was! The next year, everyone took as much as they could from me and my sister. We didn't have to say anything. After a few years my dad had us collecting up to six big bags of corn! Demand had become insatiable. Eventually, of course, we stopped going to the Glencoe plant. But the neighbors still called, wanting to know where their free corn was! The whole neighborhood had developed a sense of entitlement. I immediately saw the danger in offering people high-quality products for free. People do not respect you if you offer them something for free.

I remember eating that great tasting corn at dinner, how butter melted on the large kernels and how I salted the giant treat. Dinner time was when my dad would tell his best stories. One of his favorites was about heart transplant surgery pioneer, Dr. Norman Shumway, who was trained by Dr. Owen Wagensteen along with my father and Dr. Christiaan Barnard.

It was from my dad's stories that I learned the art of well-placed exaggeration. My dad was an artist, and all artists have to distort reality. It is these flaws and imperfections that catch the imagination. Imperfections provoke meaning.

My dad loved stories about heroes. He believed, with Joseph Campbell, that a hero is just like you or me. At some point, there is a crisis during which the hero has to make a decision. That decision and the determined discipline and pursuit that follow, transform the average person into a hero.

My dad loved Norman Shumway. While chomping on a corn cob, with butter dribbling down his chin, he would describe Norm as a maverick. Norm had the bad habit of being late and was also amusingly irreverent toward anything Dr. Wagensteen did. One time, Norm, very late for surgery rounds, rushed down the great hall of the University of Minnesota Medical Center, tripped, and fell over a patient. "Don't worry madam," he said. "We will be operating on your heart in the morning."

Dr. Wagensteen called Norm into his office and fired him; he told him to get out of medicine, and stated unequivocally that Norm would never have his support. As my dad told it, this was when Norm decided not to be beaten. "It was at this point Norm rose to a hero," he said. "We celebrated his departure as if he were a great Roman General cast off unfairly by Cesar." Within a day, Norm loaded up his entire family and their belongings in a VW Beetle van. He drove around the circle in front of the Medical Center with everyone cheering him on and declared, "I will prove to Owen Wagensteen that I am the greatest surgeon that ever lived!"

After that, Norm could only get a part time job as an emergency room doctor on the graveyard shift. One night, a patient with internal bleeding was rolled in. Norm called for the surgeon and then proceeded to gown up, open the person's chest, and begin the operation. Everyone stared in disbelief. The surgeon arrived and, amazed at what he saw, allowed Norm to finish the operation. Afterward, the surgeon said, "I have never seen a procedure like that before. Where did you learn how to do it?"

Norm replied, "I have never done it before. I just made it up. It seemed like the right thing to do." My dad finished this story by saying that in later years Dr. Wagensteen, who had fired Norman, had wanted him out of medicine, and declared he would never support him, always said Norman Shumway was the greatest surgeon he had ever trained, and the one that he was most proud of.

Granted, this story isn't completely factual, but this never mattered to my dad. It was a story!

It was like Twain or Hemmingway! The point my dad wanted to make was: If you always stay true to who you are, no matter how dire the situation, it will work out. If you stay true to yourself, you just might walk away a hero. When I would visit home, my dad would stop me and say, "Son, never let them take who you are away from you." He said that to me many times.

My dad lost a lot of weight the year he died. When he finally went to see his doctor he received very bad news. He was diagnosed with esophageal cancer. A week or two went by before he wanted to see me. He went through a crisis phase and it was only after he decided what he was going to do and how he was going to spend his last days, that I was allowed to visit him.

He didn't complain. He didn't feel entitled to anything. He didn't even ask that I be there for his final hours. He left that decision to me. He wanted this time to be comfortable and yet nothing special. But everything carried the weight of importance. I could see him observing everything even more intently than he had before. Resigned to the fact that his life was coming to an end, he set an example of how to deal with the inevitability we must all face—dying.

We went through the process on his terms. We couldn't go down the sentimental road, at least not for very long. We couldn't tell him how much we loved him, because he would dismiss it. We had to come up with other creative ways to show him we loved him. He showed us how much he loved us by hanging on to life for a couple more months, then a few weeks, and then a few days, and then a few important hours. Finally, after he waited for the perfect time to tell us his final words, he said over and over again, "I love you all. I love you all. I love you all."

He had waited for a time when it had become almost impossible for him to speak, when he was at his weakest—a time that would require his greatest strength to make his last words most deeply remembered. He wanted to etch into our minds his most important truth, "I love you all."

How will you be remembered?

CHAPTER 1

The Jerk

The worst disease which can afflict business executives in their work is not, as popularly supposed, alcoholism; it's egotism.

—Harold S. Geneen

I was in the fourth grade at Middlebrook Elementary school in Golden Valley, Minnesota when I walked from Miss Asp's class to my afternoon break on the playground. I had paused just outside of the door of the building to look out over the playground. Something had changed. The teachers, and even the principal, were treating me differently, but I wasn't accepting it. I was just watching, observing, and thinking as I watched the other kids play. Several weeks prior, for whatever reason, I had decided to actually concentrate on my Iowa test. I scored the third highest in my grade at the school.

This was unusual for me, as I had a wandering mind. These days, this behavior is considered unacceptable by a lot of parents who might reach for medication; but in my case, it was me just being a kid. I didn't know how to use my brain so I was reckless at the controls. During that test I was very quiet, focused, and I enjoyed what I was doing. Everything seemed very logical and easy for me on that test day. And thank God I wasn't medicated!

My outstanding performance was highly unexpected because I had always been placed in the slow learners group. So, it was odd when the teachers took an interest in me as if I was smart! I was convinced the teachers had me confused with someone else and were unwilling to accept the change in their treatment of me. And, before too long, they gave up on me. I was extremely DAMmed up.

My teachers didn't understand that my way of thinking wasn't stupid, it was actually very intelligent. I still couldn't understand why there was a "k" in know, which should be pronounced *k-now*, and why "know" sounded different in a word like knowledge, because it should be pronounced *no-ledge*! I had always been very logical and if I couldn't find a logical argument for something, I just wouldn't learn it. In fact, this logical way of thinking is my motivation for developing the theory of the thinking DAMs. The thinking DAMs are an attempt to logically explain highly illogical behaviors of people within business organizations. My unwillingness to compromise and accept illogical rules led me to fail one spelling test after another, but it also defined a large chunk of my identity—my ego.

I could not spell very well, pronounce words correctly, or read very well; partly because I am nearsighted, and partly because of the somewhat bizarre way I was taught to read. I think there is something to be said for an adult teaching a youngster how to read the good old fashion way: by sitting down with a child and having the child read to the adult. And that was the burden my parents had with me since I wasn't learning how to read in school. Sadly for me,

Middlebrook Elementary was a school that prided itself on being progressive. At Middlebrook, we were subjected to the mechanical reading machine. It would project single words at various speeds. It was dizzying and almost made me carsick. There was a piece of metal with a slot cut out that went back and forth to show one word at a time. It clicked and clacked, back and forth, and notched down noisily as it went to the next line. I hated the sound. I couldn't see the words because of my nearsightedness. When I got my new glasses and could see the words, well, I just saw words! I didn't understand the meaning. What I saw was, "quickly, Jack, around, here, the." Nothing made sense to me! I didn't realize I needed to see the words together in order to read and comprehend. When tested on what I read using the machine, I would never answer the questions correctly. It was just a multiple choice guessing game with me. I thought almost everyone in the class was superior to me.

I was actually very smart but because I didn't learn the same way the other children learned, I thought I was dumb. Additionally, I didn't think of myself as very athletic, which also proved to be false. From the age of three I took swimming lessons. My parents wanted to be absolutely sure I wouldn't drown in one of the 10,000 lakes in Minnesota. By the time I was eight, I was on the AAU swimming team, (the "A" team) and the top team in Golden Valley. That team was coached by Mr. Miller, who many years later, won the state High School championship with many of the swimmers from my team.

I started out as one of the slowest swimmers on the team. With each passing year, I progressively improved, but I didn't notice my speed and endurance growing by leaps and bounds; I didn't realize that I was building an extremely athletic body while I learned about focus and sheer discipline. I didn't think it was a big deal that I swam and held my own with these extremely talented athletes.

The definition of an athlete at my school wasn't someone who could swim quickly back and forth in the pool for hours, but someone who could throw a baseball or shoot a basketball. And I couldn't catch or throw anything very well.

Anyway, there I was walking out of my fourth grade class onto the playground and, as I watched the children climbing like monkeys, swinging back and forth, playing foursquare, and hitting the tether ball around the pole, I observed something. I said to myself, "There are three kinds of people in this world. There are the ones who are really smart, but have no athletic ability whatsoever. Then there are the ones who are really dumb, but have great athletic talent. Then there is me. I am both dumb and uncoordinated. I, it appears, am special." And, with a sigh, I started to play with the other kids.

This fundamental insecurity drove me to overcompensate. My typical day as a high school junior consisted of the following regimen: get up at 4:00 in the morning, run four miles, have breakfast at the school, study, go to homeroom, eat a short lunch, have concert band practice (the top band at my high school and one of the best in the state), run another seven to ten miles after school, do my homework, practice my trumpet and piano, go to bed, wake up, and repeat. On Friday, this schedule was filled with competitions and musical performances. At the time, I had no idea that what I was doing was very special. I just assumed anyone could do it.

That proved to be a problem for me in my early adult life. I could not evaluate myself honestly. As a result, I couldn't evaluate others honestly either. I judged people harshly for not being able to do what I assumed was easy to accomplish. Because of my inability to see reality, I wasn't fair to myself and I wasn't fair to others. I judged everyone with an unrealistic yardstick that elevated me above them and temporarily satisfied my need to feel superior.

This unrealistic yardstick caused problems in many areas of my life. For example, I remember taking out a former cheerleader from my high school the first year I was in college. She was very nice to me and agreed to play a friendly game of tennis with me. I, on the other hand, had the sole intent to show her how vastly superior I was, that I should be a pro, and that I should go to Wimbledon and win it! I didn't realize she wasn't having much fun. I just thought she was admiring my splendid shots: short and deep, high and low, all fast. I thought her look of confusion (or was it pain?) meant she was completely bedazzled by my remarkable talent and power. I felt great. I won every game. I was a complete jerk!

However, as you might imagine, romance didn't happen for us. She told me two things. The first was, "Gray, you aren't Mr. All American!" and the second was, "Gray, don't take this the wrong way, but you seem to have a very good relationship with yourself."

I wasn't a great teammate either. I wasn't encouraging. I wanted to demonstrate superiority. I would compete against the team in an attempt to prove that they were completely and utterly hopeless and that I was the only one capable of doing anything. As a result of my bad behavior, I made my team weaker, not stronger.

I see this a lot in corporate teams today, from the floor or shop level all the way up to the executive suite. In the DAM thinking world, everyone thinks competition is good. But, competition creates DAMs and DAMs inhibit the ability to realize potential. Competition manifests itself from an Ego DAM: the desire to be better than another. Competition is a way to prove that dominance. A team that competes against itself is not a team; it can never be a team. And yet so many companies still preach competition within their teams.

As a young person trying to learn how corporate America worked, I carried a strong competitive spirit with me. And with it, I carried my trusty yardstick to see if people measured up to my grade.

I felt that competing with others was the only way to win in the corporate world. It became obvious to the people at Norplex/Oak Inc., that I needed to be fired or sent off somewhere to be broken and put back together again. They sent me off, not to the Army, but to Dale Carnegie training. The class I attended was in Rochester, Minnesota.

If you haven't been there, you may have heard of Rochester, Minnesota. It is where the world famous Mayo Clinic is located. But more importantly, Rochester, Minnesota is smack dab in the middle of farm country. It is a place where telling people how great you are and how you are better than them doesn't always work out. The locals have a certain way of bringing you down to size.

Let's say it's winter. You get a flat and you are stuck on Minnesota Highway 52. If you demand this or that or the other thing (especially if you compound it by telling everyone how superior you are), the residents of Rochester will let you sit out in the cold. Finally, once you're half-frozen, you will simply and sincerely ask for help and they will be there with a cup of coffee for you. Uncle George will put a new tire on your car and brother Fred will fill your tank with gas and before you go, you will enjoy a home cooked dinner back at the farm. When it is −20° with a −70° wind chill, you need people like that to help you! Being arrogant is not a good strategy if you expect to survive the winter.

The cold in Rochester is the great leveler of the Ego DAM.

No matter the weather, people in farm country have a way of cutting you down to size if you stay long enough. And they love telling stories about how they did it, too. If you brag about this or that someone might say, "Come here son, I want to show you something. See that piece of glass over there. Do you know what that is? That is a mirror. Now, don't mind me. I want you to continue talking just like you are right now. Now look into the mirror while you are talking. Good. I am going to mount this mirror right up here and you can continue talking to it. I have some work to do now, and I'll be seeing you, but you just go on talking. Don't let the fact that I am not here stop you."

The instructor I had at Dale Carnegie School was a senior manager at IBM's Rochester facility up the road. And what I described with the mirror is what he figuratively did to me, class after class. He changed my life and I am forever grateful. And so, on the last day of my Dale Carnegie class, a young man who was near my age said to me, "Gray, the first time you came here and I had to listen to you, I thought you were a complete, arrogant jerk. But now, during these last couple of days, I realize you're not that bad. I might even tolerate having lunch with you sometime."

A lot of people confuse having a big ego with having an Ego DAM. If you are a corporate CEO, an executive, or a general manager of a large division, you have to have a big ego. You have to be very secure with yourself. You have to be extremely confident. Jack Welch, the former CEO of General Electric, has a very large ego but he doesn't have an Ego DAM. He asks anyone for help if he thinks they can help him or his company. Larry Bossidy, the CEO of AlliedSignal when I worked there, was the same way. He had a very large and intimidating ego, but he didn't have an Ego DAM. He assembled a stellar team, members of which went on to be CEOs of Raytheon and American Standard. A universal pattern for these great leaders is that the people they drove hard, the people that had to meet their standards, the people that they led, became lifelong loyal friends. You don't see people with Ego DAMs surrounded by a bunch of strong and capable, loyal friends.

It is okay to have a big ego. We all need one. Your ego is good. It is a gift. It brings value to others and to your company. It is something you alone develop. It's good to be very confident and secure with yourself as long as you know asking for help isn't a sign of weakness but a sign of strength. It is when we have an Ego DAM that we find ourselves in trouble. The Ego DAM comes from insecurity. A fear that people might find out we aren't as great as everyone thinks. We may feel a need to pretend that we are someone else so others will admire us and love us. An Ego DAM makes us expend energy to demonstrate how we are important, how we measure up, and how others fail to make the grade. That is why people with Ego DAMs have their own yardsticks, so that they can measure others to confirm their superiority. CEOs with Ego DAMs typically experience a high rate of turnover in their companies.

I knew someone who was promoted to a CEO position. This company's board of directors knew this CEO was green, so they offered him help. This CEO's Ego DAM first became apparent with his treatment of the consultants. The CEO would hire them based on other's recommendations. After a while, he would pull out his trusty yardstick because he was tired of being told what to do. After all it was *his* company! So, he would find a flaw and then fire a consultant over it. He would do this over and over again. Each time he used his yardstick, it seemed to make him feel better about himself. His insecurity again became apparent after he hired someone to manage sales. He got his yardstick out and asked himself, "Was a sales manager essential?" His conclusion, "No, not essential; I can do it," and he fired her. Then he moved on to the general managers. Out came the yardstick again! The general managers became his excuses for nonperformance. If things went badly, his answer was to execute one of the general managers. This jerk CEO would not take accountability and that is where serious trouble always starts for a company.

When this lack of accountability continues, the CEO's delusions and power trip grow. Reality slips into the rear view mirror. He will ascend to become Caesar of his empire—a Rock Star. His only purpose will be to decide the life or death of an employee—thumbs up or thumbs down—and take as much out of the company coffers as he can. Leaving the company in ashes is of no concern to the Rock Star. So many boards of directors believe they need to pay a CEO a huge salary or they will not attract a good one. My contention is that most companies' board of directors wouldn't hire a good CEO if they saw one! The high salary attracts, at the least, a jerk. And the rich bonuses, which have nothing to do with job performance, ensure the jerk turns into a Rock Star monster who then sacks the company for everything.

The Ego DAM is where a lack of accountability in a CEO is hatched. It is what terrified Harold Geneen. The Ego DAM is the engine. The money is the fuel. The bigger the jerk, the greater the money, the faster your company gets to its destination: Hell. When you think of Angelo Mozilo of Country Wide, Bernard Madoff, the former chairman of the NASDAQ, and Ken Lay of Enron, don't you just want to say, "jerks!" or something worse?

How many times do we have to play this movie before we learn? What is Jim Collin's book, *Good to Great* about? It's about not hiring a CEO who is a jerk. What does Bob Sutton say in his book, *The No Asshole Rule*? Don't hire jerks for any position. What does Harold Geneen say in his book, *Managing*? Egotism is the great plague of business leaders. Want to hire a great CEO? Then learn to recognize the Ego DAM and don't hire a jerk. Need a fast, almost foolproof way to find out if a potential CEO is a jerk? Take them out on the golf course. If they have never played before make them play anyway! You quickly learn whether he or she is a jerk or not.

Golf! When I first started to play, I would either hit the ball to inevitably hear it splash in a pool or watch it slam it into someone's window and break it. I quickly learned I needed help, and fast. Learning how to hit the ball well was a very slow process for me. As I moved from the driving range back onto the course and started playing with other people, I began to realize they weren't having much fun with me. I wanted to demonstrate that I was a better golfer than they were. I had all the characteristics of someone with an Ego DAM! For goodness sakes, I wasn't Jack Nicklaus at the Masters, I was Gray McQuarrie at the local public golf course. What was I thinking? I really thought people cared about how good I played. I really thought they would bow down at my feet if I hit a shot that bounced onto the green and rolled into the cup. I even dreamed of being club champion, where a great statue of me would be constructed. What a complete fantasy.

One day, while I hopelessly swung away within a deep sand trap and jumped up and down as the golf ball rolled back in, a golfer just stood there and watched my antics and hysteria. After a while he simply said, "Do you really think anyone here cares about your score?" and walked away. I stood there for a while considering his words. I hit the ball calmly out of the sand trap. I started talking to the other players. A great weight had been lifted off my shoulders: Nobody cared about how well I hit the ball or what my score was. Today, when I hit a ball that ricochets hopelessly into a wooded forest, I walk on, drop another ball, and think how lucky I am to be out playing golf. How lucky I am to be me!

CHAPTER 1 SUMMARY

People with an Ego DAM are jerks. They can't help it. They are insecure. They need to pretend they know what they are doing. In fact they will carry a yardstick of their own making to measure you and demonstrate how you are inferior. Yet they are the ones with the problem. They are the ones who won't ask for help. They are the ones creating an unproductive environment. If you work long enough in the Ego DAM culture created by jerks, you will adapt and become a jerk, too.

If you think you have an Ego DAM and want to change, consider this scenario. If you see your partner hit his golf ball into the woods, quietly help him find his ball, say little, and pretend the errant shot is no big deal. If he asks how he can stop hitting balls into the woods give him the phone number of a good golf instructor. If you mock, ridicule and try to tell him everything he is doing wrong, then you have an Ego DAM and you are a jerk.

People with healthy egos have good understanding of self. A healthy ego is a big, confident ego and others often mistake the confidence for arrogance. A confident person asks for help when he needs it. When you are open to asking for help and accepting who you really are, you will find pressure, stagnation, and pollution leave you. Little things like hitting the golf ball into the woods won't bother you or slow you down.

ARE YOU A JERK?

Instructions: Find a partner for this; it should be someone you trust will be honest with you. If you don't use a partner, it will be difficult or impossible to answer these questions honestly. First, fill out the answers independently and then come together to share the scores. Tell stories that support your position when there is disagreement or divergence. If you get emotional during the discussion, guess what? You have, at the very least, an Ego DAM.

Record your answers and ask one other (honest) person to record their answers as well.

1= Never 2= Seldom 3= Sometimes 4= Usually 5= Always

➤ Is work a race where you want to show you are better than anyone else?

1   2   3   4   5

➤ Do you hate listening to others and their stories, especially their golf stories, but like doing the talking?

1   2   3   4   5

➤ Do you avoid asking for help because you are afraid of showing weakness or of being mocked?

1   2   3   4   5

➤ Are you a jerk to others (mock them, make condescending jokes, don't offer help, talk behind their backs, make them look bad, or demean them, etc.)?

1   2   3   4   5

➤ Do you enjoy being a jerk?

1   2   3   4   5

➤ Is it impossible for you to receive too many awards, recognitions, and attention?

1   2   3   4   5

➤ Would you freak out if someone below you got promoted above you?

1   2   3   4   5

➤ When people ask, "How are you doing?" do you say you are doing great when you are not?

1   2   3   4   5

➢ Is there anything worse or more humiliating than losing?

1	2	3	4	5

➢ Do you think people care about your golf score? Really?

1	2	3	4	5

19 or below

You are in good shape, and don't have much of an Ego DAM. This means you are comfortable with people who do things better than you. You are confident in your own abilities, and you feel secure enough to ask for help from anyone.

20 to 39

You have many of the elements associated with an Ego DAM. You need to change your thinking and this will change your behavior. You need to stop seeing people and what they do as competition. People will help you if you ask and you will find that with their help you will become more productive and reduce the amount of stress around you. If you have been suffering from an Ego DAM, initially you will be afraid to ask for help because you think you might be mocked or ridiculed. If you are in a healthy environment you will be pleasantly shocked at how people will help you. If you are ridiculed, realize you aren't the problem-they are. You need to figure out how you can move on and get away from the jerks in your life.

40 plus

You're a real jerk, aren't you? Are you happy with how things are going? If not, consider a different point of view. Consider your life without your current position and status. Imagine yourself with some dreadful disease. As you imagine this, do you see yourself asking for help? If you do, that's great as you are on your way to breaking your Ego DAM. No matter what, someone will always be better than you. Refusing to admit this will just make your life, and the lives of those around you, miserable. One reason you may be such a real jerk is because the people you work with and the people you are trying to impress (like your boss) are jerks too. And if you ask for help from a jerk your biggest fear, of being mocked, will be realized. You need to identify whether you are just a jerk or you are a jerk because of the people you are working with. Make a decision to change yourself or change your work environment.

ARE YOU WORKING WITH JERKS?

Instructions: You want to find a partner for this, too. If you have a problem asking for help with this, guess what, you have an Ego DAM! Not only do you need to be aware of what is going on inside of you, but realize we adapt to the environment around us. This section will help provide insight based on the environment *you have chosen* to work in. Yes, it is your choice where you work and what you do.

Record your answers and ask one other (honest) person to record their answers as well.

1= Never 2= Seldom 3= Sometimes 4= Usually 5= Always

➢ Is work a race where others will do anything to get ahead?

| | 1 | 2 | 3 | 4 | 5 |

➢ Are you forced to listen to others who have little patience listening to what you have to say?

| | 1 | 2 | 3 | 4 | 5 |

➢ Are people in your company unwilling or scared to ask for help?

| | 1 | 2 | 3 | 4 | 5 |

➢ Are people in your company jerks who demean you and others and talk about people behind their backs?

| | 1 | 2 | 3 | 4 | 5 |

> Is being a jerk a good thing at your company?

$$1 \quad 2 \quad 3 \quad 4 \quad 5$$

> Is everyone showing off their cars, their toys, their kids, and their awards?

$$1 \quad 2 \quad 3 \quad 4 \quad 5$$

> Do people freak out at the idea of someone beneath them getting promoted above them?

$$1 \quad 2 \quad 3 \quad 4 \quad 5$$

> Do people have a hard time admitting what isn't going well for them and instead say and pretend everything is great?

$$1 \quad 2 \quad 3 \quad 4 \quad 5$$

> Are people completely humiliated when they lose at something?

$$1 \quad 2 \quad 3 \quad 4 \quad 5$$

> Do people brag about their golf score and handicap?

$$1 \quad 2 \quad 3 \quad 4 \quad 5$$

19 or below

Count your lucky stars, because this result is rare. You work in a company that doesn't have a culture full of jerks! If you are unhappy at work, don't even think about calling that headhunter to see if you can find another job somewhere else. I have had a number of friends who, early in their careers, left good companies only to work for bad ones and then regret it for decades. If you find yourself unhappy in a company like this it could be because you have an Ego DAM. You are the reason for your own unhappiness, not others.

20 to 39

Don't despair yet. Almost every company has some form of an Ego DAM culture. It's just a question of how far up the pyramid your company is. For now, realize you will have to show by example that asking for help is a good thing. When people ask you for help, don't follow the accepted company culture and be a jerk. Go out of your way to help those that ask. If you aren't careful you may find that you have started a subculture in your company and you, through your behavior, have become its leader!

40 plus

Well you might be right to despair a little. Companies with this strong of an Ego DAM have other DAMs too. You are likely frustrated. You need to study what is going on around you in terms of the DAMs. Use this book and listen and observe. What other DAMs are around? What would your company be like without all of these DAMs? Write it down. Keep a journal, starting now, and write in it as you read this book. Also, start talking to people and keep an eye out for a better company.

CHAPTER 2

The Perfectionist

---

*Striving for excellence motivates you; striving for
perfection is demoralizing.*

—Harriet Braiker

People who create great buildings, come up with great inventions, and develop great products, are not perfectionists. They are imperfect and flawed persons just like all of us and so are their great works and contributions. Joseph Campbell, author of *The Hero with a Thousand Faces* said it best:

Out of perfection nothing can be made. Every process involves breaking something up.

If these great works were truly perfect, and the people who created them were perfect people, no idea, no new method, no new construction could be derived from these achievements because, *out of perfection nothing can be made.*

It's strange that we consider flaws to be bad things when actually they make room for further growth; it is also strange that we reach for perfection not realizing that if we actually achieved it we would stop growth in ourselves and in others, now and in the future.

Perfectionism is the result of stacking the Learning DAM on top of the Ego DAM. Perfectionists have no need to ask for help because they know everything. They have nothing new to discover. They are perfect. They have no need to grow, nothing to change.

If you took a poll, most people would say being a perfectionist is a good thing because we think of it as maintaining high standards of quality. However, the perfectionism I am referring to isn't about maintaining high quality. It is about deluding oneself and trying to hide flaws. It is a mask. Perfectionists are afraid of being themselves. As a result, they experience pressure, pollution, and stagnation. A perfectionist has a DAM problem.

It is very easy to confuse someone who has extremely high standards, is dedicated and driven, and at times extremely un-compromising, with someone who is a perfectionist. Perfection-ists are all about appearances. They care about what other people think. It is very easy to spot true perfectionists because they can-not take criticism and they refuse to learn. Criticism is really an offer to help. The Ego DAM blocks a person from accepting help. Criticism is really an offer to consider another person's ideas. The Learning DAM blocks a person from accepting another person's ideas. Criticism is unacceptable to a perfectionist.

Many people think Lance Armstrong is a perfectionist. I don't and here's why: Lance has been very creative in both his life and his professional athletic career. He has flowed from being a cham-pion tri athlete at the age of 16, to a time-trial specialist in pro-fessional cycling, to a seven-time winner of the Tour De France. People who reinvent themselves are FLOW thinkers, not DAM thinkers. To reinvent yourself you have to be able to ask for help and take criticism; you have to be willing to experiment, fail, and learn. Lance Armstrong is about reaching out and asking for help. Nothing about him is about hiding his mistakes!

You don't have to look far to find Lance's opposite. Jan Ulrich, also a cyclist and the leader of Team Telecom, comes to mind. Jan was considered by many to be the most talented and gifted cyclist who ever lived. Expectations for his career were huge, and some people were already ordaining him the greatest cyclist ever, after he won his first Tour De France. Jan had great success but never really lived up to expectations. Why?

Jan was a DAM thinker. First, Jan had an Ego DAM, especially when it came to beating Lance. He thought he could beat Lance with sheer will and he believed that superior talent would always prevail.

Second, Jan had a Learning DAM. He wouldn't change his in-efficient style. He insisted on staying in a big gear as he ascended the Tour's unforgiving climbs. It was an incredible display of strength but the application was unnecessary and horribly inef-ficient. A child could see it. Everyone wanted to scream, "Jan, go into an easier gear! Get up and out of the saddle!" This is what we want to say to perfectionists when they are struggling.

Jan wasn't competing with Lance. He wanted to win the tour in some perfect way that was etched in his mind. And there was no changing Jan's mind. Jan Ulrich was competing against history; he was competing against all the cyclists yet to come; he was compet-ing against the entire universe. Ulrich lost every time to Lance in the Tour because his obstinate focus blinded him. He will always be remembered as second to Lance Armstrong.

Perfectionists create unrealistic expectations that ensure their failure before they even start. For a perfectionist, it is not about being the best—it is about being perfect. No two goals could be more dissimilar. No two goals can produce such different outcomes.

Perfectionists can be incredibly successful people or complete failures. Because perfection is unattainable, all perfectionists believe they have failed. The great Leonardo da Vinci seems to fit that mold. Consider his statement near the time of his death,

> *I have offended God and mankind because my work didn't reach the quality it should have.*

For us mere mortals, that statement simply does not compute. It is a complete disconnect based on what we know he accomplished. Clearly, he must have had an Ego DAM because he expected to be perfect so that only God was worthy to judge his work. It's hard to imagine Leonardo having a Learning DAM but history is filled with his unfinished works, works that fell apart because he failed to consult with the experts of his day.

Contrast him with Michelangelo. Whereas Leonardo was trying to prove his worth to God, Michelangelo believed that his ability to create beautiful things flowed through him, from God. Michelangelo was moved by divine inspiration, not to prove he was better than everyone, but to honor what God gave him. He wrote…

> *Every beauty which is seen here below by persons of perception resembles more than anything else that celestial source from which we all are come…My eyes longing for beautiful things together with my soul longing for salvation have no other power to ascend to heaven than the contemplation of beautiful things.*

Where Leanardo was obsessed with achieving the perfect paint stroke, working methodically and carefully on something on a much smaller scale like the Mona-Lisa, Michelangelo worked frantically to release the 17-foot tall figure of David from the rock. Working freehand, without models or sketching on the rock, the only thing that guided him was the image he had in his mind—an image that didn't belong to him, but to God. You see this free-flowing style in Michelangelo's unfinished works known as "The Prisoners," in the Galleria dell' Accademia in Florence. The exposed portions of the figures looked as if he merely peeled the rock away. You can't work this way if you worried about being perfect.

Unlike Leonardo, that Michelangelo had mentors and teachers is well documented. He was constantly learning and asking for help from others. Michelangelo knew what he wanted and went for it. The Sistine Chapel's frescoes read like a modern-day political cartoon, lampooning the pope and the corrupt policies of the church. When Michelangelo painted the Sistine Chapel it was really an act of defiance. The painting had nothing to do with achieving perfection. It was an attempt to condemn the church and live to tell his friends about it. In fact, Michelangelo actually hated painting. He was a sculptor.

Michelangelo wasn't perfect. His most famous statue—the Pieta that is housed in St. Peter's Basilica, shows a crucified Christ in Mary's arms—and has big flaws. Hands and bodies are distorted almost to the point of being abstract. But we don't see the flaws and obvious distortions because Michelangelo studied the Greeks and their use of distortion in depth. The Greeks used flaws and distortions to make the Parthenon appear perfectly flat and square, with columns of equal height and diameter. Nothing could be further from the actual truth.

Perfection is an illusion. Michelangelo knew that. He certainly didn't apologize for the quality of his work or convey any disappointment to God. We respond to what appears to be perfect. Ironically, flaws can actually make something appear to be perfect.

In our highly competitive world, perfection may seem necessary, but striving for perfection will only damage you. I knew a CFO who prided herself on being able to look into anything and anyone and pull out all of the flaws. In fact, that was a large part of her job, since her background was as a forensic accountant. Her problem was she worked in almost complete isolation. She couldn't lead others in important initiatives. She couldn't hire and retain people to work under her. Her employees didn't like her pointing out their flaws. But if you want to lead people, you have to appreciate and work with their flaws. I'm still not sure if it was the job or her personality that created her perfectionist mindset.

At Norplex/Oak Inc., after my Dale Carnegie experience, I was given the assignment of dealing with Rockwell Collins of Cedar Rapids, IA. I was to be their technical service go-to person. Rockwell Collins makes all of the stuff in a jet plane's cockpit that make it an intelligent machine, and they were having a problem with our laminated, glass reinforced, Teflon material. At this time I still had an Ego DAM. I thought I could present perfect plans that had every possibility and contingency covered. Nobody could have any input to MY plan because it was perfect! In fact, nobody could say no to MY plan because it was perfect! My Ego DAM was about to be delivered a serious blow, right there in the middle of Iowa— God's country.

Teflon by itself isn't very solid, it moves and deforms. Since it isn't very stable, it has to be reinforced with something. At Norplex/Oak, that something was woven fiberglass. The problem was Teflon doesn't stick to anything, including glass. The people down at Rockwell had to take this laminated, fiberglass reinforced, Teflon material and be able to drill it and plate it to make printed circuit boards. When you drilled into this material, the fiberglass would pull out of the material like thread from a sweater. And when you plated these damaged holes, chemicals would soak into the material like a sponge. This was a problem.

The first time I went to Rockwell I wanted to fix this problem. I talked to their drilling engineer, Forrest Voss, and... and explained what I wanted to do, in perfect technical jargon. Having created such a perfect presentation, I was sure he wouldn't be able to say no to me. Once I finished flawlessly proving my point, I closed my mouth and awaited his, "Yes, of course Gray let's do it" response. He looked up and simply said, "I don't want to do it." He turned to his desk and started working as if I wasn't there. Silence. What could I say? Free will? He had a choice. My Ego DAM just couldn't deal with the simple reality of his obvious choice, "I don't want to do it." With his words echoing in my brain, I stumbled out the door like a drunk, got in my car, and headed for the all-you-can-eat cafeteria just down the road. I needed comfort immediately and I got it. Iowa has some of the best comfort food around!

Each week that I visited Rockwell, the same thing happened. I would tell Forrest what I wanted to do and he would say, "I don't want to do it." After many attempts, during which I got absolutely nowhere, I tried a different approach.

"Forrest," I said, "I don't understand a whole heck of a lot about what you do with this Teflon material. I was wondering if you could *help me* understand how it is processed in your shop. It would really *help me* understand how I can *help you* and the other engineers."

"Fine," he said, "come back after lunch."

I later learned that after lunch was the time when he could give me his full attention. He walked the floor with me and I watched him do his job, soaking up as much information as I could. Unknowingly, by closing my mouth and listening to Forrest, I was building his trust in me. By asking for his help I was surprised, if not shocked, at how much he was willing to help me. This was my first sip at the reservoir of help that is out there if you are willing to ask for it. It was my first taste of how people forgive your flaws, if you ask for help.

After a month, Forrest wasn't just helping me understand the process; he was getting involved in my life. He was asking me all sorts of questions about my background: my parents, my sister, my beliefs, what mistakes I made, my relationships. Opening up to Forrest and letting him in seemed mandatory, like some sort of ritual. I couldn't, at first, put my finger on it until I remembered the ritual on the playground. The stories we would tell, one kid to another, to decide if we were going to be friends or enemies. I wasn't sure if opening up to Forrest was the right thing to do, but I didn't care. I liked it. It seemed to help me. He seemed to understand I needed a lot more help than just learning something about his process or doing a specific study!

In time, Forrest became like an older, bigger, wiser brother. We were like family, a good family, where we watched each other's backs. My visits became something much more important than work. They were about memories, life, and having a true friend; about learning, growing, listening, understanding, and about becoming a better person. I learned that Forest wouldn't trust or work closely with anyone who wasn't his close, trusted friend, period. And he wouldn't give you the time of day or lift a finger for you if you were a jerk. He would be polite and tell you, "I don't want to do it." It is just the way it is done in God's country! If you pride yourself on being perfectly professional, you just aren't going to get very far.

One day he started *talking*. It turned into a story about a young lady from Dupont who came and taught Forrest how to collect data and analyze it using a process called Design Of Experiments (DOE). Together, they discovered how to get the most out of the Dupont material. What was previously a mystery now became obvious to me. The only way I was to get his cooperation was if the

DOE effort was his idea, not mine. It became clear that I must be the one following Forrest, even if it meant deviating from my idea of how the DOE should be conducted.

Once our goals were in sync, we worked productively with each other and produced constructive results. Together, we published and presented a paper at a major industry trade show. And one day, a year or two later, a colleague called me and explained that we had been wrong; our reasoning had been flawed, and he had come up with a better way.

At the time, I was irritated. Today I am proud. I am proud of the flaws in our study that were clearly described in our paper, because they proved to be something valuable *from which others could build.*

CHAPTER 2 SUMMARY

Out of perfection nothing more can be built; there can be no more advancement. Perfection defines the stopping point. Perfectionism is the Learning DAM stacked on top of the Ego DAM. The perfectionist can't ask for help, this is the Ego DAM. The perfectionist can't learn and discover anything new, this is the Learning DAM.

People with exacting standards, who are highly demanding, are often thought of as perfectionists, but they are not. They are constantly experimenting, always striving to be better. Perfectionists do just the opposite. They wait for the perfect time, a time that never comes. They don't change. They use the same approach again and again.

What most people don't realize is that a seemingly perfect work, be it a building, a sculpture, or a painting, isn't perfect at all. It has flaws that make it appear perfect. Perfection is an illusion. People respond to flaws. People isolate themselves when they try to achieve perfection. People are deterred when perfection is demanded. People ignore perfection if it is presented to them; if they can't interact with it, who wants anything to do with it? The pursuit of perfection needs to change into the pursuit to be better.

When you can surrender your Ego DAM and your Learning DAM you will find that the velocity, quality, and emergence of your life will improve dramatically. When you can ask for help, be open to others and their opinions, knowledge, and experience, you will be affected in a positive way. You will change. You will grow. And you might find a true friend you can share many great memories and stories with for the rest of your life. It is amazing what perfection blocks if we choose to demand and pursue it.

ARE YOU A PERFECTIONIST?

Instructions: You want to find a partner for this (always). Learning can't happen in a vacuum. We can't learn and grow perfectly by ourselves, even though we might like to. Fill out the answers independently and then share your scores with your partner. Confused? My instructions aren't perfect enough for you? Ok, let me be clear, your partner is grading you only. If your partner wants to be graded, tell him or her to go buy my book! As you can see these are very imperfect and unprofessional directions. By the way, what did you do today? Oh, yes, the instructions. Remember to tell stories to back up positions when you disagree. Good luck!

Record your answers and ask one other (honest) person to record their answers as well.

1= Never 2= Seldom 3= Sometimes 4= Usually 5= Always

➢ Is no job ever done well enough for you?

| | 1 | 2 | 3 | 4 | 5 |

➢ Do you expect others to apologize when they are not perfect?

| | 1 | 2 | 3 | 4 | 5 |

➤ Do you hate receiving advice?

1   2   3   4   5

➤ Do you want people to say, "It's perfect" about everything you do?

1   2   3   4   5

➤ Are you reading this book looking for all of the typos and grammatical errors?

1   2   3   4   5

➤ Do you pride yourself in knowing you can always find flaws so you can condemn the person or use it against them to your political advantage?

1   2   3   4   5

➤ Do you like to use the word "perfect" to describe yourself, your life, your children, your work, your expectations, or anything you organize or do?

1   2   3   4   5

➤ Is there only one way to do something…the one and only perfect way? And does this way happen to be your way? Just curious.

1   2   3   4   5

➤ If someone misspells a word do you think they are an idiot? (By the way, are you finding misspelled words in this book?)

1   2   3   4   5

➤ Is it vitally important to you that you be perfectly professional when dealing with people in business?

1   2   3   4   5

19 or below

You are in good shape and you are lucky. Trying to be perfect can make your life miserable. Since this isn't the case, because you arrived at this score with your partner (tell me you didn't do this yourself, because if you did you wasted your time) then you are comfortable asking people for help. You are comfortable saying you don't know or don't understand something. You want to discover new things. You understand your flaws and know you are far from perfect. You see the flaws in others, but can work with them and be maximally productive. You don't expect things to go perfectly or people to perform perfectly or that everyone will say "yes" to you because what you said was perfect. Perfection's only guarantee is misery. Stay away from the perfection concept.

20 to 39

You see perfectionist tendencies in yourself. Congratulations! You are being honest with yourself and this is your first step toward being better. If you scored low on being a jerk but high here, you have an Ego DAM operating. The reason this didn't show up before was due to my imperfect questions written in this most imperfect book. But you have an Ego DAM and let me explain why. You are being blocked by your motivation to be perfect because you need tangible proof that you are better—or the best. That is an Ego DAM. Want to fix this? Ask help from others. Invite them to tell you about your flaws. Don't argue about any of this; just listen. When you do, you will find the pressure to be perfect start to diminish.

40 or above

You are very honest. Congratulations! Did you score high for being a jerk too? Was it tough finding a friend who would be honest with you on this? People don't like hanging around with people who demand that everything being perfect. There is probably some fundamental reason for your need to be perfect. Admitting imperfection probably feels like falling off a cliff to you. Get some help. Ask for help. Listen. Then go to the golf course and don't get frustrated by any shot you make. Have a friend keep score. The score they keep will be the number of times you complain or become frustrated with your shot. When you have a lot of people who want to play golf with you, then you will have moved away from being a perfectionist. Don't play golf? I didn't say these recommendations were perfect. Improvise. Figure out something else where someone can keep score. Build on top of this very imperfect section with these very imperfect ideas. And for goodness sakes, have fun.

ARE YOU WORKING WITH PERFECTIONISTS?

Instructions: With your partner (who you trust and isn't perfect) score the people you work with. Are you confused again? Are you expecting perfect instructions? Look, think about everyone and try to generalize in some way. Your partner doesn't work at your company or with the same people? Hmmm. Is that required for a perfect score? Is it required to learn? Are you going to give up, or are you going to find a way your partner can help you evaluate the people you work with? Lots of holes here aren't there? Perhaps you have created your own process here; possibly you've even deviated from my instructions. What will this create? Learning? Discovery? Anyway, fill this out with your partner (independently or not) and find a score that you both agree is the right score (not the perfect score).

Record your answers and ask one other (honest) person to record their answers as well.

1= Never 2= Seldom 3= Sometimes 4= Usually 5= Always

➤ In your company, a job well done is never good enough.

1	2	3	4	5

➤ Where you work, do people expect you to apologize for not being perfect?

1   2   3   4   5

➤ Are people at work extremely defensive and reluctant to admit they are less than perfect?

1   2   3   4   5

➤ Do people want you to say about whatever they are doing, "It's perfect," and nothing else?

1   2   3   4   5

➤ If you were to give this book to others in your company to read, would they focus on the content or obsess over the typos and errors?

1   2   3   4   5

➤ Do some key managers in your company pride themselves on their ability to find flaws in anything and use this ability to their political advantage?

1   2   3   4   5

➤ Do you work in a company where bosses and managers use the word "perfect" a lot and expect you to use it too?

1   2   3   4   5

➤ Do people in your company preach and believe there is only one right and perfect way to do things?

1   2   3   4   5

➤ Do you have many people in your company who like to read something and then point out all of the misspellings and grammatical errors as if they are incapable of making such errors themselves?

1   2   3   4   5

> Is it expected in your company to look perfect, to speak perfectly, and to wear really nice shoes, otherwise your career won't advance?

1   2   3   4   5

19 or below

This score indicates you should be really happy to be working for your company. A company that doesn't expect perfection will forgive you for making mistakes and will allow some latitude to do things your way. It is a place where you don't have to be professional all the time and is likely a company that will even allow fun! In fact, if your company expects you to make mistakes and rejects entirely the idea of anything that looks like perfection, well, you must be working for one of the top performing companies in the world.

20 to 39

You are working for a typical company. If you scored low on being a perfectionist you are likely frustrated. You know your company could be more productive. You know your company could enjoy more important discoveries that would propel it into a leadership position ahead of its competitors. A company with a perfectionist culture is a company that is starting to age. It is becoming less flexible about new ideas. It is typical. Keep your eyes open for better companies and better opportunities. No need to jump ship yet.

40 or above

If you scored low on perfection or you want to fix your perfectionist leanings, you need to quit this job soon! It will wreck you. Day to day pressures probably feel sky high. You probably have developed very bad habits to manage your stress. You likely doubt yourself and are full of worry. It doesn't take many DAMs (two here) to create an intolerable working environment for people, where being unhappy is the norm. If you don't get out, the situation will start to degrade your physical and mental health. It isn't worth it. Life is short. Summon all of your power and ask for as much help as you can to get out. Keep in mind there is no perfect way out. There are many options that could be right for you. Have the courage to do what is right for you and your family.

CHAPTER 3

The Righteous

---

*I am indeed amazed when I consider how weak my mind is
and how prone to error.*

—Rene Descartes

I always feel pressure, see stagnation, and experience pollution when I am around righteousness. A righteous perfectionist jerk is truly a very difficult person to be around, let alone live with!

Divorce rate statistics in America are disturbing: 50% of first marriages, 67% of second marriages, and 75% of third marriages end in divorce. This data suggests a huge Learning DAM, because previously married couples don't seem to learn from their first and even second marriages! What they seem to have learned is how to divorce!

This also suggests people aren't asking for outside help. We know this is an Ego DAM. If you think there isn't anything new to learn because you already know everything about being married, we know that is a Learning DAM. If we see the marriage as ours to control, as ours to have, as "my precious," we know this is the My Precious DAM. When you stack these three DAMs you have what I like to call a self-righteous, perfectionist, jerk. Others have noticed this stacking of behaviors too. As I combed through a marriage counseling web site, www.*wordofloveforyou.com*, I found this quote ...

"*Self-righteous perfectionists are the hardest people in the world to live with.*"

The danger with righteousness is it can lead to fanaticism. The fanaticism of the Spanish Inquisition led to thousands of deaths. The fanaticism of the Nazis led to millions of deaths. The fanaticism of the Khmer Rouge gave rise to the term *killing fields* and nearly wiped out an entire people. When you need to be right or be righteous, take heed: evil starts with perfection; evil manifests itself in the need to be righteous; evil opens the door to fanatics who will cleanse the world of the infidels.

I have seen too many employees have too strong a need to be righteous. And I have seen too many good people get fired or leave because of self-righteous fanatics! The need to be right, without going through a process to find out what is the truth, seems so innocent that we often overlook it and don't bother to challenge people who are righteous when we should. We would prefer to remain polite. We would prefer to resolve a disagreement without conflict. This is a fantasy. This is the feelings DAM in action.

Righteous people wreck businesses. Unfortunately, very few people can even spot a righteous person over someone who is right. Instead we prefer to categorize people as polite or impolite. We want polite people in business and what is right and wrong is a matter of opinion. This is the road that will lead all companies to disaster. When business leaders challenge their people about what is and isn't right, what is and isn't the truth, then you get a great product like the Macintosh Computer and a great company like Apple. This more than anything was Steve Jobs' gift to the world: his never-ending quest to find the truth and do something right. Why was Jobs fired from Apple? It wasn't because he wasn't right; it was because he wasn't polite.

What does it mean to be righteous versus being right? I want you to stay put and physically not move. Do not go outside or Google or call a friend to find out the answer to this next question. Does a road sign such as a "Do Not Enter" or "Slow," or a speed limit sign or green highway sign have square corners or rounded corners? Close your eyes if you have to visualize and remember. Write your answer down. How strongly do you feel you are right? Absolutely 100%, or not sure? If you feel you are absolutely 100% right could someone convince you that you were wrong? If someone disagreed with you and argued passionately that they were right and you were wrong does that make them righteous? Is agreeing to disagree the right thing to do, because it is the polite thing to do?

Steve Jobs argued passionately that his team was wrong and he was right when the team wanted square corners for the graphical windows displayed on the computer screen. It was critical that the graphical user interface be intuitive and be aesthetically pleasing and these were "must haves." Jobs position was, square corners were well outside of human experience. The team's position was, square corners were well inside of human experience. Who was right? What was the truth? Jobs would not listen to any of their arguments. It was a waste of his time. It was a waste of the team's time. Why? Because he knew he was right, because he had already done tons of observational work. Is it fair to give others equal hearing no matter what? Yes. Is it right to give others equal hearing? No.

Is business about being fair? No. If you don't have the facts and have not made careful observations about a situation it is best to keep your righteous judgments to yourself and shut up and listen.

Steve didn't listen to any counter argument. He simply dragged his lead programmer Bill Atkinson outside and had him start counting rounded corners. It became obvious who was right. The next day Bill devised a way to have Mac windows displayed with rounded corners!

If you find a person unyielding to your position they could be righteous or they could be right. You start by doing your home-work and research to discover what is the truth; only then can you differentiate who is righteous. Righteous people will think all road signs have square corners even after you show them the facts. Righteous people will think Gray is not my name, but a color, even after they are presented with the facts.

I am very attached to my name—Gray.

It's a unique name. Note the letters and their order. 'Gray' is different from 'Grey' or 'Gary' or 'Greg.' But a lot of people, who hear me say my name, don't think I said it right!

For example, when I say, "Hi, my name is Gray," I often get back "Nice to meet you, Greg."

Over the years, I've learned to move things along. I say, "Hi my name is Gray—Gray, like the color." I have developed many variants of this such as, "Gray, like my personality" or, "Gray, like your grandmother's gray hair." The person inevitably pauses and ponders this before saying, "Gray, hmm…unusual name…I think I like it."

Without fail, a few hours later, the same person will be back to calling me Gary. When I correct him again, he says, "Oh no, you misheard me, I said Gray."

This is said with conviction and confidence that I will believe it. And I will—right up to the point where the person starts calling me Gary again! The mistake happens because the person calling me Gary has grown up knowing that Gary is a name for a man and Gray is a name for a color.

The problem with the need to be righteous is that it buries the truth. When we are righteous we believe a rule without question. The truth is secondary. We are unwilling to change or consider anything that violates our rule. Sometimes we need certain beliefs in our lives that we accept on faith, areas where we will not accept any challenge. But if rules dictate our entire lives, we are in trouble. And believe it or not some people will never accept that my name is Gray, because it is wrong. Why? Because it just is. Like a religion!

Are they right? Were my parents wrong? What do the facts say? What is the truth? According to the US Census Bureau, Gray, as a first or second name, is the 665th most popular name in the US. In fact, there are almost 80,000 people named Gray.

Despite this fact, there are yet more righteous beliefs about this name. Some people are of the opinion that Grey is the correct spelling and Gray is an incorrect variation. I have encountered many people who won't budge from that opinion because to them, it isn't an opinion, it is a self-righteous viewpoint that they can't let go of. It is their *My Precious* rule! Who is right? And what is the truth? Of course, the truth really doesn't matter to the righteous.

Let's continue. Gray can be spelled two different ways: G-r-e-y and G-r-a-y! The general convention is that G-r-e-y is the English version and G-r-a-y the American version. But is this convention consistent? No. There is the well-known Grey Rock Inn in Northeast Harbor, Maine; and there is the town of Grays in southern Britain. In the United States there was a popular TV show called *Grey's Anatomy*! The famous anatomical book, after which the show is named, is *Gray's Anatomy*. Who was the author of this great book? Henry Gray. And where was he from? You guessed it, Britain!

Our opinions, judgments, and made-up rules aren't right very often. Rene Descartes said, "I am indeed amazed when I consider how weak my mind is and how prone to error." This man invented the Cartesian coordinate system and modern day analytical geometry that made it possible for others like Newton and Leibniz to invent the Calculus. He is credited with being the father of Western philosophy and the author of the famous phrase, "I think, therefore I am." He is considered the last man to have all of the knowledge of the entire world in his head! He knew everything there was to know! And yet, he questioned himself. He knew that if he relied strictly on what was in his head, he was prone to error. Prone to be wrong!

Righteous people believe they can never be wrong—ever. To be wrong creates a crisis they can't handle. For some people in Japan, it is such a dishonor to be wrong about important things that they commit seppuku, or harakiri, also known as ritual suicide, ritualistic suicide. Why? Because this tradition has been annealed into Japanese culture like a Samurai sword. In Japan, people kill themselves over failed businesses, love triangles, and even for failing school examinations. Many people in Japan prefer death over living a life of dishonor. A righteous belief system can trap and doom us. Learning, unfortunately, is not an option for the righteous. Righteous people may be intelligent, but they are not smart. And when confronted with facts that contradict their beliefs, if they don't choose suicide, then they live a life of delusion, devoid of reality or facts.

The alternative to this madness of pretending we are right, when in fact we are wrong, is to apply the scientific method. When using the scientific method, there is no need to be either correct or right at the beginning. You just present a theory or an opinion and test to see if it is true. If there is a single observation that violates the rule implied by your theory or opinion then it is invalid. It isn't true. No big deal; no dishonor; no jumping off a building. Learn and move on.

The difference between science and religion is science is never certain, while religion is always certain. That means that all the evidence supporting the truth today could be found to be wrong tomorrow.

Many CEOs have strong opinions. Often their proclamations about how the world works become the unquestioned religion of the company. This makes any company rigid and susceptible to crisis. And yet this obvious fact is ignored; it is not even taught in our schools. I recently had a chat with a young person who wanted my opinion about what college they needed to go to. I asked this young person, "So you know what the word dogma means?" Now, mind you, this is someone who could get into Stanford or any school they want. They had never heard of the word! This word is so important to understand, I feel obligated to provide the definition.

Dogma is the established belief or doctrine held by a religion, or by extension by some other group or organization. It is authoritative and not to be disputed, doubted, or diverged from, by the practitioners or believers.

I asked a second question, "Why do you want to go to college?" The answer, "Because that is what I need to do to become successful?" Since this person wanted to be successful in business, I then asked, "Can you be successful in business without having a college degree?" The answer, "No." I asked, "Did Steve Jobs have a college degree?" The answer, "Yes, because you can't be successful without a college degree." I asked, "Does Bill Gates have a college degree?" I got the same answer. I then asked, "Does Charlie

Shipley have a college degree?" Now I got a blank face. I said, "You need to look up the word dogma. Because of your dogmatic beliefs you don't have an open mind that is ready to learn. College would be a waste of money for you. If you go to business school and then run a company you will ruin it."

When I worked for Shipley Company they had two facilities. The older one was in Newton Lower Falls, MA. The other, which was impressive, sat on a quaint, wooded hill in Marlborough, MA. On my way to Shipley's Marlborough headquarters I drove by huge, sprawling buildings spaced around the rolling hills. All the buildings were owned by Digital Equipment Corporation (DEC). It was an impressive campus and was just one of several large campuses that DEC inhabited. At that time the VAX, a mini, mainframe-like computer, was DEC's primary product and was responsible for DEC's huge growth. In fact the VAX stole huge market share from IBM.

About that time, DEC was faced with an impending crisis— one it hadn't seen coming. The threat was sitting on my desk at Shipley in the form of a small Apple Macintosh computer. This small computer would soon have as much computing power as DEC's VAX at a fraction of the cost. And the reason behind this was due to the work occurring within Shipley's walls! Not many people at DEC even realized, much less appreciated, what Shipley was up to.

Few people have heard of Shipley or understand the significance of this company in our lives. Today, it is a very profitable division of DOW and it is called DOW Electronic Materials, yet the name Shipley remains on many of their products! And people in the industry still refer to the Shipley name when thinking and talking about their products. This says a lot about the legacy that the Shipleys left behind.

The power of a microchip is defined by how many transistors can be crammed onto a small piece of silicon. To make these transistors you need a photographic material, much like film in a camera, called a photo resist. The resolution of this resist defines how small you can make the transistors. Shipley invented the positive photo resist and continued for decades to provide higher resolution resist products for its customers, like Intel. Shipley *enabled* Moore's law, which states: The power of a small computer chip doubles every two years. To give you an idea how important Shipley Company was to the semiconductor industry, Charlie and Lucia Shipley won the SEMI award for the invention of the positive photo resist. They were the third recipients of this award. They followed the inventor of the process for ultra-pure crystallization of silicon and the inventor of wafer mapping. Shipley's invention was fundamental and essential for the growth of the industry.

I am taking this sidetrack to make an important point. Charlie Shipley did not have a Ph.D. in chemistry. In fact he didn't even have a college degree. He took just one chemistry course at Yale. Was Charlie Shipley successful in business even though he didn't have a college degree? By any measure, yes, he was. Shipley created great products. The company created a great business model. They established an entirely new industry and were extremely profitable. Rohm & Haas spent a fortune to acquire Shipley Company. And DOW spent a fortune on Rohm & Haas—largely because of the Rohm & Haas acquisition of Shipley Company.

Would someone from DOW hire a college drop out like Charles Shipley today? No! Would they make such a person, with no track record, head of a new business unit to invent a new industry from scratch? No! They would hire someone from a prestigious graduate school with a Ph.D. degree in physics or chemistry or both. Someone who has experience at Lawrence Livermore

National Laboratories or Bell Labs; who possibly teaches at a prestigious college or university, or has a prestigious position at IBM, Intel, or somewhere else; who has published hundreds of papers and belongs to a long list of academic and professional societies. Why would they do this? Dogma!

I witnessed Mr. Shipley hire such a person to lead Shipley's research and development department, to lead the next generation of innovation at Shipley. I remember being in that person's office. It was large, fancy, formal, intimidating, and uninspiring. When you entered his domain, it was clear who judged your work, who judged your ideas, and who judged your future. It was all about self-righteousness: the power to judge and condemn. It was about one man who was always right, and he had the credentials to prove it! His space felt lonely.

By contrast, if you could find Charlie Shipley's office, a closet-sized space tucked into the back of a lab that was piled high with books, bottles, and flasks, you would find him working on something—always. He greeted you warmly and sat down and spent time with you. You quickly became wrapped up in his childlike exuberance that was always glowing in his eyes. He clearly loved each and every day and loved what he was doing. If you made the effort to find him he was going to reward you with a story. When I had the chance I would take a friend to meet him in his lab. No appointment was ever required. Just stop in and hunt him down. These two different worlds, the open-minded and the closed minded, clashed; the VP didn't last.

Few companies can innovate, especially big companies. The accepted myth is an unwillingness to take a risk! This isn't the problem—ever. When a company thinks they need to find the smartest, most self-righteous person they can to lead their research and development effort is when a company can't innovate anymore.

The righteous want to be strong and they want you to be dependent. The righteous want to be in the know and judge what is right, while leaving you in the dark. The righteous want you to believe that what they have is an ordained gift, which you can never posses. Maintaining this illusion provides the righteous infinite security and infinite value to your business. If you present them with facts that demonstrate they are clearly wrong, be aware you are attacking them personally. They may say, "Who are you? An insignificant bumblebee?" And they would tell a person like Charlie Shipley why the bumblebee can't fly! And then they would grab their can of Raid!

On Charlie Shipley's office door was this simple quotation by Mary Kay Ash:

Aerodynamically, the bumblebee shouldn't be able to fly, but the bumblebee doesn't know it so it goes on flying anyway.

DEC's CEO, Ken Olson, didn't know a bumblebee was working hard on products that would make the VAX obsolete. In fact, he self-righteously condemned the entire notion of the personal computer. He stated:

There is no reason for any individual to have a computer in his home.

This was a religion within DEC. It was ingrained in their culture. It was wrong and it destroyed them. By the time DEC began to dabble in personal computers (which they called microcomputers) it was way too late. And DEC's effort to build a PC fast, failed. It was as if the entire company, by failing at this effort, was motivated to prove Ken Olson right! Self-righteous leadership breeds absolute conformity.

When DEC began to collapse, I watched the buildings on its campus emptying. It was shocking to see how suddenly a company could blow up. Other companies that failed to recognize the impact the PC would have on their businesses—companies like Data General and Prime Computer—were failing as well. The human pain and suffering I saw all around me left a strong impression. This impression, in part, motivated me to understand why companies fail and what makes a company great, which lead me to the DAM thinking construct.

Many CEOs and business leaders would rather follow; they don't like to innovate. Innovation is uncertain. Repeating what successful companies do seems like a safer road to travel. The problem is you could be going down the wrong road. Just because something worked yesterday doesn't mean it is the right thing to do today or tomorrow. As soon as you think there is a right way to do things—and this right way will never change—you leave yourself open to making the same tragic mistake as DEC did under Ken Olson.

At the time the VAX design was growing, others thought Ken was right. People listened to DEC. People copied DEC. And when the world changed, they all went down together. I watched it happen. I lived it. Anytime someone quotes some important CEO who says "this" to justify "that is why we are doing it," I shake my head and say, "Yes, but is it the right thing to be doing now?"

Righteousness gets in the way of even simple troubleshooting. Troubleshooting after all, should be simple, logical, fast, and straightforward. But when righteous people are involved, it can become long, circuitous, frustrating, and messy. Let me share an example.

I have some electronic equipment in my office/studio that I use for radio interviews and podcasts. When I recently upgraded this equipment, it didn't work as expected. I wanted to talk, record, hear myself, and hear the caller. And I wanted the caller to be able to hear me too. Well, when we hooked everything up, it wasn't happening. I could hear the caller, but the caller couldn't hear me. The "expert" who sold me the equipment told me this shouldn't be happening.

He said that it worked when he set it up, and what was happening had something to do with me! I had messed it up somehow. He was extremely righteous and this proved to be massively frustrating for me. After doing some experiments, the solution became clear to me; however, the "expert" didn't want to listen to my idea.

Finally, I demanded that he come to my office and fix the problem or take everything back. After two days, the problem was found. This happened because I made him call the manufacturer who explained to him what I had tried to tell him. As I had discovered a few days before, when you plugged in a certain cable all the way, it shunted the signal away from the caller. You had to leave the cable only partly plugged in!

The "expert" was astonished, white faced, and tortured. Everything pointed at him being wrong about so many things. That it had worked when he had set it up before was only one example, because when he tested the system the other person was just down the hall. He just assumed what was being heard was through the equipment. He had decided it was going to work and failed to observe what was really happening. This happens in business all of the time. Keeping the cable plugged in half way was a simple solution to the problem, but it was unacceptable to him, because it wasn't the answer he was looking for, particularly since he didn't think there was a problem to begin with. I was the problem. And in his mind I was still his problem, because I was showing him things that were completely unacceptable. To this day, this "expert" doesn't acknowledge this solution as acceptable or that he was wrong in any way. This attitude is the classic fingerprint of someone who is extremely righteous.

Near the end of completing this book, I was having a coffee at a popular Starbucks frequented by all sorts of interesting people. A person began to talk to me , and in the course of the conversation, I found out he was a trial attorney. I started sharing with him the ideas to this chapter. He was captivated and listened to me closely. He talked to me about his DAM problem with juries. For example, in his book, Blink, Malcolm Gladwell talks about in his book, *Blink*, how we reach decisions in an instant and once we do that, our opinions become facts in our head. Our righteous beliefs stop us from further examination and critical thinking. As a trial attorney he told me jurors make their decision very quickly, within minutes. The trial is suppose to be a process that uncovers the facts and the truth, but unfortunately that isn't what really happens. It became clear that he frequently experienced the human suffering caused by righteousness. He was so passionate in this he shared with me the history of the Somme battlefield of World War I and how the righteous beliefs of British Field Marshal, Sir Douglas Haig, created a needless killing zone.

Haig had substantial experience fighting battles. Is it experience that should be valued or the ability to learn and adapt that should be valued? Most companies almost always pick the former, and this is why too many companies slip into crisis. This was the lesson Haig taught the British army as his righteous beliefs, honed by decades of experience, slipped them into crisis.

On www.history.net, in the article, "Field Marshal Sir Douglas Haig: World War I's Worst General," we see a huge learning DAM.

The man was so confident in his outdated ideas that he never allowed actual battlefield experience to challenge them.

Haig didn't think. A leader who values experience only is a leader that doesn't think. A leader like this assumes what worked in the past will work today and in the future. A leader like this isn't a leader, but a "bloody" disaster—literally.

Haig righteously believed the tactics employed by the British in the American Revolutionary war were still valid. Marching infantry troops out in neat orderly ranks with a slow advance so he could control them would create a predictable, positive outcome. Mounted cavalry on horseback would win the day. Haig didn't believe in the machine gun. He didn't have any and he didn't think much of the enemy for using them. Using them wasn't the "right" way to conduct a military operation. Apparently, thinking the German's were idiots, which is typical of someone with an ego DAM, on July 1st, 1916, in Somme France, he sent 110,000 British infantry over the top of the trench, deciding to use a strategy of attrition, to punch a hole through the German lines. In a few hours there were 60,000 casualties and 20,000 dead, all mowed down by the German machine guns. In the entire 140 day battle, not a single objective was achieved: Germany 80,000, Britain 0. Any professional coach in the NBA or NFL would have been fired long before a score like that would be posted! Did Haig learn anything from this? No.

A Haig staff Colonel wrote: "The events of July 1st bore out the conclusions of the British higher command and amply justified the tactical methods employed." Haig refused to change his DAM thinking.

He wanted more troops to assemble a larger army, so that he could do it again on a much grander scale, and get it right. He did the same exact thing again in the battle of Ypres, in Flanders, with disastrous results. Winston Churchill came to realize that,

Haig, 'wore down alike the manhood and the guns of the British army almost to destruction.'

In Haig's tragic battle for Passchendaele, British Historian J.F.C. Fuller wrote,

To persist...in this tactically impossible battle was an inexcusable piece of pigheadness on the part of Haig.

If you have any pigheads in your company you have a righteous DAM problem. The pigheads will destroy your company.

Your legacy will always be stained with the disaster, because you were there. Like the trials of Nuremberg after World War II, outsiders will wonder why you did nothing, why you didn't mutiny, why you didn't shoot the pighead.

In 2011, I spent five days in Las Vegas attending Tony Robbins' Business Mastery course with about 1,000 other people. Every morning there was a drawing. If your name was picked, you were called on stage. I didn't think there was any chance my name would be called. One morning we were all cheering and hollering. Team 5, sitting a few rows in front of me, was called. I was part of Team 19. Then I heard something strange, "Gray, Gray like the color! Are you here?"

I thought, Gray like the color? That has to be me. I used this phrase so many times when I introduced myself that it was strange to hear it from somebody else. The day before, I gave the announcer my book and I may have even said, "My name is Gray, Gray like the color." I suspected that stuck in his head—as I ran for the stage!

While the stage hands thoroughly checked my name tag, my teammates looked like the deer caught in the headlights. I'm sure they wondered, "What is he doing on stage? He isn't part of Team 5!" One Team 19 member even rushed up to try to get me off the stage. When that failed, she demanded to see the ball that clearly said "Team 19, Gray."

I wound up winning the trip to Fiji to attend Business Mastery II. As I walked back to my seat I expected happiness and congratulations from my team. What I got instead was a cold welcome. They asked, in a very confused sort of way, "Weren't you with us, Team 19?" "Well I heard my name, and that is why I went up there," I replied.

It took a long time for them to accept the fact. When we are convinced we are right in the moment, because we believe so strongly in the accuracy of our mind, without examining and analyzing the facts, we behave righteously. Some people on Team 5 never accepted the facts. They believed, and told me so, that somehow I was a thief. They were so confident in their belief! Yes, it hurt a little and it was a little frustrating. I knew there was little I could do. Their minds were made up. They were, to put it bluntly and impolitely, pigheads like General Haig.

CHAPTER 3 SUMMARY

To be righteous is to be right, no matter the truth. If the truth contradicts the belief, the righteous bury the truth. It's about the power of being the only one to judge what is right and what is wrong. It's about absolute control of a specific domain, territory, department, or company. Nobody is allowed into the decision making domain of the righteous. This is the my precious DAM. In order to bolster control of the domain there is an ego DAM ("I am better than you"), followed by a learning DAM, ("there is nothing you can tell me, because I know it all"). Righteous people are intimidating and that is their intent.

Righteousness has killed a number of great businesses. Consider the CEO who thinks the general population has no need for computers. What about the executive in charge of research and development who believes he has nothing to learn from others? From the young person who feels she has to go to college to be successful, to the hightechnology company that believes only people with advanced degrees can be innovative, or the military general who believes unquestionably that the methods of the past will work in a future battle. Their closed minds and righteous beliefs choke growth. If you want to kill innovation in your company, hire a righteous executive. If you want to inspire innovation, hire someone who has a burning desire to do something great and wants to get it right, like Steve Jobs. You want to hire the guy who has the burning desire to get it right in their heart and not the guy that knows he is right no matter what.

It can be dangerous for any company to take what has made them successful and create a dogma around it. Always use the scientific method where all assumptions, beliefs, and theories about the business are tested to see if they are, in fact, still true. If you don't do this your business will not be able to improvise, innovate, or adapt to the changing, flowing world around it. You will be left with a wrecked business and people who have to rebuild their lives. What a legacy!

ARE YOU RIGHTEOUS?

Instructions: Find a partner who will not judge you in a righteous way. Do you righteously believe that righteous people should be condemned, or fired, or removed from your life? Well if you do, you are righteous too. Righteous people are closed minded. Open-minded people can improvise and innovate. How can you let a righteous person in your life in a way that is creative? More importantly, how can you help them to become a better person if they admit to you they are struggling and ask for a little bit of help? That is the ultimate test to determine if you are a DAM thinker or a FLOW thinker. Anyway, answer these questions and use your partner as a coach so that both of you agree on the answers here. Good luck.

Record your answers and ask one other (honest) person to record their answers as well.

1= Never 2= Seldom 3= Sometimes 4= Usually 5= Always

➢ Do you explain how things should work and disregard how they actually work?

1   2   3   4   5

➤ If someone disagrees with you do you reach for the can of Raid so you can kill them like a bumblebee?

1   2   3   4   5

➤ Do you think you have to go to college to succeed in business?

1   2   3   4   5

➤ Do you judge a person's business acumen by the type of shoe they wear (if you aren't wearing Ferragamos you feel naked)?

1   2   3   4   5

➤ Do you feel if what you tried didn't work you should do it again in exactly the same way until it works like Field Marshal Sir Douglas Haig?

1   2   3   4   5

➤ Do you reject the scientific method, because it's a waste of your time and besides you already know the answer?

1   2   3   4   5

➤ Do you judge people harshly when people change what they are doing instead of sticking with the original plan?

1   2   3   4   5

➤ Do you impatiently listen to people, because you are waiting to tell them what they need to do?

1   2   3   4   5

➤ Do you enjoy judging anything and finding faults (admit it, it's fun)?

1   2   3   4   5

➤ Is it your vast experience that makes you so valuable to your company (it's cool when you don't have to think anymore and don't have to adapt and change)?

1   2   3   4   5

19 or below,

Outstanding! You realize that your opinions aren't fact nor are they the truth. You realize that you might be wrong. And being right isn't that important! Congratulations my friend. Do something special for yourself today. You are going to be very successful in this life! You have no idea how rare of a person you are. You are willing to be challenged because you know this will maximize learning and produce new discoveries. You use the scientific process in order to find the truth. You know the world changes and you can flow and grow by adapting to it.

20 to 39

Congratulations on being honest. What to do? First, have you discovered that, at times, you are a jerk and a perfectionist? Second, do you realize that you are expending a lot of energy trying to prove you are right? Try listening more and talking less. Ask questions. Consider others' opinions and viewpoints. And for at least a month, never interrupt another person no matter how difficult this may seem for you. Listen carefully and pretend your brain has been wiped clean of all information like a computer memory chip or pretend you are like an innocent new born baby who doesn't know anything. What is right in what they say? How do you feel about it? How could the truth be uncovered? And realize, once it looks like the truth is uncovered, this too could change! This too could be proven wrong!

40 or above,

I don't know how you have made it this far into the book. First, my book has to seem wrong in its content, in its writing, and in its style. Perhaps the only reason you are reading it is so you can tell me why each chapter is wrong. However, if you want a better life, hopefully what I am saying will start to sink in for you. Spend a day, or a week, or a month, just asking people questions and listening. But I want you to do something else too. I want you to go find a righteous person like you that has just the opposite belief. And I want you to endure the person for a month, working closely with them or taking them out to lunch a couple of times a week, going to their church, going to their meetings, and completely immersing yourself in their world. And you can't say a thing or make any judgment about them. Keep your mouth shut and listen and observe. Allow them to judge, but do not judge them. I guarantee you this will change your life! If you can survive these two seemingly simple tasks, there is hope for you. And read the rest of the book. It will help too you.

ARE YOUR COLLEAGUES RIGHTEOUS?

Instructions: Find a partner who is open-minded, who will not judge you in a righteous way. Go through these questions and think about your group of colleagues as a whole. What are they like? When pressured, how do they behave to maximize their safety and security? We all adapt in order to survive. Our work environment strongly affects how we behave at work.

Record your answers and ask one other (honest) person to record their answers as well.

1= Never 2= Seldom 3= Sometimes 4= Usually 5= Always

➤ Do others explain how things should work and disregard how they actually work?

        1   2   3   4   5

➤ Does everyone spray each other with Raid because they always need to be right?

        1   2   3   4   5

➤ Do people in your company insist on hiring people with advanced degrees and from prestigious companies, only?

        1   2   3   4   5

➢ Do others judge you by the type of shoe you wear (better figure out how you can get those Ferragomo's slipped into an expense report)?

$$1 \quad 2 \quad 3 \quad 4 \quad 5$$

➢ Are people in your company completely learning disabled like Field Marshal Sir Douglas Haig?

$$1 \quad 2 \quad 3 \quad 4 \quad 5$$

➢ Do people in your company reject the scientific method because they already know the right answers and have better things to do?

$$1 \quad 2 \quad 3 \quad 4 \quad 5$$

➢ Do people stick with their original plan when it has become obvious the plan is wrong?

$$1 \quad 2 \quad 3 \quad 4 \quad 5$$

➢ Do you work in a company where people very rarely ask questions, but instead tell you what to do and judge you?

$$1 \quad 2 \quad 3 \quad 4 \quad 5$$

➢ Do people enjoy judging anything and finding faults in your company?

$$1 \quad 2 \quad 3 \quad 4 \quad 5$$

➢ Do people brag about their years of experience again and again endlessly?

$$1 \quad 2 \quad 3 \quad 4 \quad 5$$

19 or below,

This low score for a company, as in the previous two chapters, is rare. You have a lot to be thankful for. If you find yourself being self-righteous when working for a company like this, you should consider changing, stop judging, and become more open-minded.

If you got fired you deserved it and I salute your company for understanding that behaviors lead results!

20 to 39

Many companies are like this. Part of the reason is most companies don't know what productive behavior is—FLOW thinking—and what unproductive behavior is—DAM thinking! We are taught to tolerate bad behaviors but not bad performance. The message is, "I don't care how you do it, just get results." It does matter how results are achieved. Enron, Worldcom, and AIG showed us that! See how the political tide is moving. What kind of leader is your boss, your boss's boss, or your CEO? Get yourself invited into their working space if you can. You can learn a lot about whether the company has a righteous culture by just listening and observing. Give a righteous person, who has trust in you, a copy of my book. Have a discussion. See if you can start to create zones in your company that encourage openness and experimentation. Good luck!

40 or above,

What can I say? Quit, unless you truly enjoy working there. But, don't be surprised about a crisis that suddenly wipes out your company and your job.

CHAPTER 4

The Entitled

---

*The best way to find out if you can trust somebody is
to trust them.*

—Ernest Hemingway

What's wrong with an entitled leader? Do you have one in your company? Do you trust them? Do they trust you? Do they motivate you? Or do you want to go find another job?

I once had a CEO say: "Gray, I ask myself this question every day. If I gave everyone in my company a gun and a knife, then turned out the lights, would I live?" My first reaction to this strange query was, "I would never think of a question like that." My second was, "Hmm, I wonder what would happen if I had his job? Would I live?" And my third take was, "I think I have to get away from this guy, because this is a really bad way to think."

You can't lead without trust and you can't receive trust without working at it and earning it. If you side step this work—because you feel entitled to have your employees kiss the ring on your hand, do what you say because they fear you, work day and night sacrificing their personal life and health—you will fail. You will create a company with employees who distrust you and may even hate you. They just might use that theoretical gun and knife if given half a chance.

Before you take out your yardstick and harshly judge people you think are entitled, take stock of yourself. Almost all of us have some area of our lives where we feel entitled. For example, if you lost a loved one, were fired from a job, or didn't get the promotion you expected, you would experience loss and anger. You might be angry with God, your boss, or your company. You might lose trust in what you believed. Why? Because you believed you were entitled to a specific outcome and didn't get it. When reality collapses a person's *entitled* vision, the Ego DAM supports the bitter thoughts, "I deserve it, not you." The Learning DAM blocks the ability to discover new opportunities: "I know it all and I don't need to listen to your advice." The My Precious DAM keeps the pain close and others out: "You couldn't possibly understand how I feel, so butt out." And the Trust DAM blocks communication: "I am unwilling to trust anyone anymore so I am not talking."

Tragedies and crises happen. They have nothing to do with the kind of person you are, they have nothing to do with your belief in God, they have nothing to do with making your parents or wife or boss happy, and they have nothing to do with how wonderful your children are. They don't have anything to do with your healthy lifestyle, how much money you have, or your political affiliation. Ultimately, we are all dead men. How we deal with this reality defines our character and humanity.

When you feel that what happened in life isn't fair, consider Vladimir Lenin's attempt to make everything fair all of the time! Was it fair that the bourgeoisie didn't work? No! So Lenin took all of their property and the property of every citizen away in an attempt to make everything fair. No ownership by anyone of anything. This is the end game of entitlement! When we want everything to be fair always, then we lose everything that we have: our freedom, our liberty, and our right to pursue happiness.

What about our capitalist system? Is it perfect? No. Is it immune to the same entitlement mentality that defined the Union of Soviet Socialist Republic? Sadly, no. Too many young people have a huge sense of entitlement. They see "gangsta" rap stars driving around in fancy cars; they see "Jackass" movies where the stars make hundreds of millions of dollars; they see talking faces on late night TV telling them they can walk to their mail box and pick up a check without doing anything. Anyone can have a ton of money. It is easy. In fact, work for pay is dishonorable. We are entitled to the good life so just give me that million dollar McClaran, and I'll take that now, if you don't mind!

What does this have anything to do with business? Who you hire to work for you represents a cross section of the culture your company is in. I remember spending some time in the small country of Montenegro, an extremely beautiful country on the Adriatic Sea. Montenegro was part of the former country of Yugoslavia, which was part of the old USSR. Talking to the delightful young people there a few years ago, they had very little motivation to work for private companies. Why? Because they thought they were being "molested" for expecting to work for pay! They thought it was outrageous that they should have to work 30 hours per week, when they were entitled to get paid for food and basic shelter for doing nothing.

Here in the United States it is bad, too. The goal of many young people is to get rich quick without having to work. It's about not having a boss and being your own boss. It is about selling gold coins, or miracle creams, or diet pills, or telephones, or health juice, or diet pills, all using network marketing. Network marketing isn't about the product. Network marketing isn't about building anything with people creatively. Network marketing isn't about working towards something and being on a journey. Network marketing is about easy money. And if you have to work for that money, you are a fool. When you have to hire a person with this kind of entitled view you have a nightmare, because they are an entitled, righteous, perfectionist, jerk. They will want to be paid, even when they don't perform. And this type of entitlement goes right to the top, right to the CEO! Is it any wonder why we have lost our competitive edge to India, and China, and Japan, to name a few?

It isn't just the gangsta role models that are creating an entitlement vision. It is also our very best business schools. The message is, "You aren't like everyone else. You are special. You know the answers. You deserve the huge salary. And all you had to do was get a degree from our school. You are now golden." People leave business school thinking they are ready to lead our biggest and best companies and be paid as if they have 40 years of experience! Is this right? Is something wrong? Where do DAMs come from you ask? They come from the culture in which we live. These thinking DAMs and their DAM behavior are taught to us.

I knew a CEO who had strong entitlement beliefs. He deserved his high salary, because he was a CEO with an MBA from a really good school. This entitled CEO didn't want to go through the work of leading and he was very angry with his sales organization. They had become the enemy, because in his eyes, they were threatening his high-paying job. The problem? His revenues and customer base were not where they needed to be. His solution? Get angry with them. He jumped up and down and pointed fingers. He threw up numbers, quotas, and budgets. He said bad words. He demonstrated time and time again how nobody in sales measured up. He demonstrated how salespeople were robbing his right to a high-paying job. He wanted them to know, if he couldn't pay his mortgage, neither could they, because he was going to fire all of them. Witnessing this firsthand was a horrifying experience. This CEO needed to unlearn what he had been taught in order to have any hope. He needed to *change his DAM thinking*.

A while back, I took Tony Robbins's Business Mastery course. A lot of executives think this is the guy who teaches you to walk on hot coals without burning your feet. Tony is a very smart guy and his week-long course is extremely intense and it is all about business. About three-quarters of the material addresses who you are and how you think; the rest is technical. Early in the session Tony said that you are naturally gifted in one of three business areas: 1) You are an artist; 2) You are a manager-doer; 3) You are an entrepreneur.

An artist loves to create, doesn't like to manage, and doesn't like to take any risks. A manager-doer loves to manage, doesn't like to take risks, and doesn't enjoy developing new systems, processes, or products. An entrepreneur lives for the hunt, loves to take risks, isn't an artist, and doesn't like managing. Now you may be a combination of these styles but one, two at most, predominate.

At a Robbins event, people know Tony will barbecue you if you ask a question. He knows how to help you see your real problem so you can do something about it. People who have been there know the risk, and they love it. Even though they may be publicly humiliated, they trust Tony, and know he is trying to make them a whole lot better.

An individual on our team stood up on his chair so he could get barbecued. This individual said he was the creator of a business in which he and his partner assumed all of the risk. He said they couldn't get sales going. He wanted to know what was wrong with sales people.

"I see you are an entrepreneur. You likely don't value people who just manage businesses and you likely don't value sales people, am I right?" Tony asked. The person acknowledged that this was true.

"Let me tell you something," Tony continued. "First, you think you have a sales problem but you don't. What you have is a business problem. And that is because you aren't leading your company. You aren't finding the right people. And you aren't focused on what is truly important to your business."

It was brutal! The person's facial expression was like that deer in the head-lights. I admired my teammate for standing courageously on his chair because his personal sacrifice was going to make us all better.

Tony went on, "Second, you need to become a leader. And the only way you can do that is to learn to love what you hate. If you can't do that, you may need to shut down your business and go find a job working for somebody else. What do you think?"

My teammate, almost shouting, said, "I want to learn to run my own business."

"Then you need to learn to become a good salesperson," Tony responded, "not with the intention of being the only sales person for your company, but with the intention of knowing enough about the sales job so that you can lead your sales team. If you don't understand how to do a job, you cannot lead somebody else who is doing that job. If you don't learn to love sales, you have no chance. Does that make sense?"

"Yes," my teammate replied.

Sadly, I rarely see a CEO try to unlearn their bad behavior so that they can lead in the way Tony describes. What I see instead are the fancy offices and the nice shoes and a preoccupation to talk about themselves or their toys. When they talk about their business, it is as if it is their possession. They make brash statements about their own self-importance and descriptions of what they are entitled to. Too many CEOs have been trained in balance sheets and business law and organization structure only. What all CEOs need is an examination of their lives and encouragement to become better people, so that they can be true leaders. Too many CEOs have never read nor taken to heart the quotation below with the intent of becoming a great leader...

> *"To lead people, walk beside them...As for the best leaders, the people do not notice their existence. The next best, the people honor and praise. The next, the people fear; and the next, the people hate...When the best leader's work is done they say, "We did it ourselves!"*

A CEO that can't trust and walk beside his people must lead by fear. Fear is the fingerprint of bad leadership. It is the ultimate leading indicator of a company that will plunge into crisis.

But this isn't the only way a crisis can start and spread because of entitlement behavior. I knew a manager that thought a major customer would never let him down. This manager wasn't listening to his customer. He had no reason to. All of the customers business was in the bag! He was doing his job and meeting deliveries. And because of that, he was entitled to maintain all of the business.

One day an important part number was pulled by the customer and given to the manager's competitor. The manager's trust with his major customer was lost in an instant. He started calling and making all sorts of accusations and threats to his customer. He wanted justice. He wanted fair treatment. He wanted a logical, just explanation, because he knew in this debate, he would prove he was right and the customer was wrong.

What happens when you want everything to be fair all of the time? You lose everything: your job, your company, your happiness. This entitled manager wound up losing his most important customer and threw his company into crisis. Despite how right you may be, entitlement is a disease that will kill any business. You are never entitled to your customer's business ever. You need to be very grateful for the business you have! Entitlement behavior always makes any crisis bigger and you lose even more of what you had. Making things fair is never the fix. Your best chance of keeping any customer is listening to them and asking the hard questions in order for you to get the true, hard information.

Earl Bakken, cofounder and former CEO of Medtronic, had this to say about customer relationships:

> I believe that in many cases the close working relationship between our salespeople and our customers actually reduces some of the difficult information we need to hear. By that I mean that our customers may, in many instances, be too close to our representatives to speak their minds about our products and processes. ... And it is candor—the bad along with the good—that we always must be willing to hear. ... I believe the best place for picking up the unvarnished 'truth' about our company and our products is on the customer's home turf—in their [places of work.]

Earl Bakken hasn't been leading his company for decades. Eventually, Medtronic became overrun by some of the smartest people coming out of the best business schools. I remember taking a bicycle trip in Italy where I got close to a couple of orthopedic surgeons. When I started talking about Medtronic they suddenly became silent. Then, over the course of the trip, when I had earned their trust, they absolutely unloaded about how arrogant they thought the Medtronic sales team and the executives that visited them were. If they had a choice, they absolutely would not be using Medtronic products.

Since William George, the author of *True North: Discover Your Authentic Leadership*, left Medtronic as its CEO, the value of the company has declined on Wall Street. Why? Success can breed arrogance. It can breed the Ego DAM, the Learning DAM, the My Precious DAM, and the Trust DAM. A company can get to the point that it tells a highly trained surgeon, "We are better than you, we know more than you do, we decide, not you, what is best, and we will get back to you at our convenience."

A CEO is ultimately responsible for the culture of a company. It's hard for me to find anyone that says Steve Jobs was a great leader and motivator of people especially in the early days of developing the first Macintosh computer. Yet I think he was a management genius, because he understood what his engineers needed in order to be motivated. What did he do? He told his engineers that their work was shit. What Steve was doing was part of a very specific process: *all processes involve breaking something else up.* By saying their work was shit, he was breaking all of his engineer's ego DAMs. They all were starting from the same place—zero. In order to move away from this they all had to learn to work together, which made the team increasingly productive.

It's easy for entitled executives to kill the passion in their employees. For example, when our small team won the AlliedSignal Premier Achievement Award, we were very excited. When we all flew out to Newark, New Jersey, we were picked up by an old limo that smelled and we were all crammed in it and experienced an uncomfortable ride to Morristown. Throughout the course of the event, Larry Bossidy, the CEO, didn't talk to me personally, and neither did Fred Poses, the president of the chemicals division. Mostly, it was a show of who was important and who wasn't important. The whole thing was a waste of money. The whole event made me feel my work didn't amount to much. Perhaps it was worth the $4,000 that was given to me for 50 shares of AlliedSignal stock. I left there thinking I didn't belong. I wondered where my efforts would be more appreciated.

For a lot less money, what would have had me floating on a cloud, would have been to receive a phone call from either Larry or Fred and have them talk to me and the others for a few minutes. That would have made me believe I was important to the company. This would have made me want to work ever more passionately to do an even better job.

Mary Kay Ash, in her book, the *Mary Kay Way*, explains that the exclusive role of a manager in her company is to make people understand they are important to the company. A manager that can't do that at Mary Kay is fired. As she says…

> It was John D. Rockefeller who said, 'I will pay more for the ability to deal with people than for any other commodity under the sun.' High morale is a significant factor in increasing productivity, which means that a good leader should continually strive to boost the self-esteem of every individual in his or her organization.

Let me give you an example of the hidden power that is at your finger tips. For a client, we created a tribe to improve the productivity of the plant. Part of what the tribe did was to define a reward ceremony. If someone went above and beyond to do something good for the tribe they were rewarded with a chant that said something like, "You lead not follow. You are the best. You stepped up." It was amazing how this simple acknowledgement changed the dynamic of an indifferent work force, to an impassioned work force. It was amazing how people walked away from the simple spontaneous ceremony saying, "Wow, that felt good." Over time people couldn't resist the temptation of going to work and stretching themselves a little further and doing even better work, knowing they were appreciated.

Entitled leaders fail. They use fear. Trusted leaders succeed. They create passion.

CHAPTER 4 SUMMARY

Chapter 4 is about *the entitled*. Entitlement happens when the Trust DAM is stacked on top of *the righteous*. Any hint of entitlement is bad for business and it's bad for society. Strangely, when you feel entitled to things being fair, you start a never-ending spiral of loss. The result is making things increasingly unfair for more and more people, even though the intention may be correct and the cause noble. Taken to its extreme you are left with big government distributing all goods and services equally like in the former USSR. In order to be free we have to realize life will not always be fair. Nobody is obligated to be your customer no matter how well you have treated them. No matter how well you have done your job nobody is obligated to keep you employed. The world changes, technology changes, and the economy changes. People have free will. They have the power to make choices. To think you can control outcomes and get life the way you want it, will just make you a bitter human being.

Those who consider themselves entitled operate within a fantasy realm and the denial of reality exposes them to potential disaster. The only things we can be sure of are the things that have already happened. When things change, the journey changes and the new plan that emerges may be much better for you and your business. If you choose to hold on to what you feel entitled to, life will just grind you down.

Too many executives come out of business school thinking their employees will follow them just because of their degree and their position. It has never worked that way ever in the course of human history. Great leaders must earn the respect and trust of their followers. The best way to do that is to understand their job, understand what they go through, and treat them with respect and humanity. For a leader, it isn't the education that is valuable. It is how you treat people that will make you a valuable leader. This takes lots of work and if you aren't willing to do this work, to understand everyone's job, to craft a journey and a cause that will inspire and create passion, you will never lead. Leadership has always required a lot of work. It has never been an entitlement where people follow you automatically.

ARE YOU ENTITLED?

Instructions: Find a partner. Keep in mind you are not entitled to their help at all. They have the right to tell you no if they choose. What are you going to do to increase the chance they will say yes, help you, and stick with it all the way to the end of the book? It means you have to think about them and not just yourself. Entitlement is all about you and not them. Now that we have that straight you are ready to begin. Answer the questions and use your partner as a coach so that both of you agree. And don't feel you are entitled to a partner who will tell you what you want to hear. Good luck.

Record your answers and ask one other (honest) person to record their answers as well.

1= Never 2= Seldom 3= Sometimes 4= Usually 5= Always

➤ Do you feel entitled to your job?

    1   2   3   4   5

➤ Are you mad when you don't receive something you feel you should?

    1   2   3   4   5

➤ Are you angry at a customer who leaves?

    1   2   3   4   5

➤ Would your employees shoot you, because they see you as an entitled, righteous, perfectionistic, jerk?

    1   2   3   4   5

➤ Do you think communism is a great idea, especially if you could be Stalin and make all the decisions?

    1   2   3   4   5

➤ Would you lose your faith if a loved one died suddenly?

    1   2   3   4   5

➤ Do you believe if you are good nothing bad will happen to you?

    1   2   3   4   5

➤ Do you believe your employees have to follow you, solely because you are their boss?

    1   2   3   4   5

➤ Do you feel that building trust in your company is a waste of time?

    1   2   3   4   5

➤ Do you think you are entitled to be the author of this book and enjoy all of the royalties and benefits?

    1   2   3   4   5

19 or below

You are in good shape. You have an attitude that clients, employers, bosses, and customers will appreciate. They know you will be interested in their business. They know they can trust you. And your customers know you will understand if they do business with somebody else.

20 to 39

You are operating on dangerous ground as is typical for many of us. Feeling entitled, in business or even in your own life, leads to disappointment. You must understand there are never any guarantees, even with the people you consider to be the most loyal to you. Nobody can predict the future. Nobody can anticipate what is going to happen and how things might change. Be grateful for what you have. Ask the hard questions and listen to the hard answers you don't want to hear. You need to be a better supplier to your clients and to your customers. And if you are dumped, be grateful for what you had. Things may turn out better than they would have if you got what you first wanted.

40 or above

You're honest. Your score is a step in the right direction. Realize you have some work to do to get rid of the entitled, righteous, perfectionistic, jerk, who determines your behavior. Commit yourself to building trust around you. When you say you are going to do something do it. Listen and observe and ask others how you can help. Ask for help and don't judge. Work side by side with a worker or manager or customer on something significant. Show that you care and show that you listen through your actions. After you have walked in their shoes and understand their work, think about how they want to be treated. Help them in a way that brings out their greatness. And when the great work is done, it wasn't you who did it. They will say to you, "We did it."

ARE PEOPLE IN YOUR COMPANY ENTITLED?

Instructions: Find a partner. Now I know I am not entitled to obedience. You may have decided to answer these questions yourself. What can I do…nothing. I am just glad you have read this book this far. Consider this: It is next to impossible to try to answer these questions without help. If you don't seek help, realize you have an Ego DAM. And that Ego DAM is going to prevent you from being as productive as you could be. Anyway, go ahead and answer the questions and use your partner (I really hope you have one) as a coach. Good luck.

Record your answers and ask one other (honest) person to record their answers as well.

1= Never 2= Seldom 3= Sometimes 4= Usually 5= Always

➤ Does everyone in your company feel they are entitled to their job?

1   2   3   4   5

➤ Are people mad when they don't receive something, like a bonus, when they think they should?

1   2   3   4   5

➤ Are people angry when a customer leaves for no good reason?

1   2   3   4   5

➤ If you had the chance, and were given a gun and a knife, and the lights were turned out, would you shoot your leader?

1   2   3   4   5

➤ Does the culture of your company remind you of communism? Do people get rewarded for nothing? It is all political?

1   2   3   4   5

> Would people in your company feel really mad if they were fired from their job even if they clearly don't do any work?

1	2	3	4	5

> Do people in your company pass the buck, when something goes wrong?

1	2	3	4	5

> Do your managers and leaders think it is a waste of their time to communicate with you and learn about your issues? But they are more than happy to tell you what to do?

1	2	3	4	5

> Do you feel you have to constantly watch your back because nobody trusts anyone?

1	2	3	4	5

> Have people in your company divided up into camps and become entitled, righteous, perfectionist, jerks?

1	2	3	4	5

19 or below

Your company is in excellent shape. There is trust in your company. Entitlement erodes trust. Remember there is potential for entitlement especially when things don't go according to plan. Your company is probably a fantastic place to work with a fantastic leadership team. In my opinion you are a fool if you want to quit and leave. Or you feel entitled to more (which means you are still a fool.)

20 to 39

Many companies are like this. They often have an entitled, righteous, perfectionistic, jerk in a leadership position who makes a potentially fantastic place to work, just average, or worse wrecks it. So what have you done about it? Have you thought, that is just the way it is and accepted it? If you have, you have let your own internal standards slip. You are adapting to the company culture. And in the end people will start to lose trust in your ability to perform and meet commitments. You need to either see if you can help change the company or take your time and find a much better company to work for.

40 or above

I can only imagine what it must be like working where you work. Do everything you can to do your work and isolate yourself from all of the entitled people. Construct a plan to leverage your position so you can find a better position in another company. Staying too long will negatively affect your mental and physical health. No amount of money is worth that.

CHAPTER 5

The Rock Star: All Hail Caesar!

---

*You ask me if I have a God Complex. Let me
tell you something. I am God!*

—Dr. Jed Hill from the movie Malice

"*Et Tu Brute?*" These famous words were spoken by Shakespeare's Julius Caesar when he realized even his best friend wanted him dead. Until he was murdered, Caesar truly felt he knew what was best for Rome. The senators couldn't figure out how to control Caesar's ambition so they did the only thing they could think of—they killed him.

The God Complex, or what I like to call the Rock Star, incorporates all of the Thinking DAMs. It is the Feelings DAM stacked on top of the Entitled. As a result of having a Rock Star in your company, the entire purpose revolves around satisfying the feelings of the Rock Star. When this happens you have lost control and your company will experience a slow, agonizing death.

Rock Stars will work their way into everything to show you how indispensible they are. They will make others their slaves. They will start to whisper that they, not you, run the company. They will tell anyone who will listen about their credentials, how they are the experts, how they are making the decisions, and how they are the only ones who know what is going on. If this reminds you of anyone in your company, you likely have a Rock Star.

There is a scene in the movie *Malice* that has all of the elements of the Rock Star. What is bizarre about this scene is, if you aren't careful, you walk away thinking Dr. Jed Hill is someone you need! People with a God Complex are very persuasive.

The scene is as follows:

The question is, 'Do I have a God Complex?' Which makes me wonder if [you] have any idea as to the kind of grades one has to receive in college to be accepted at a top medical school; if you have the vaguest clue how talented one has to be to lead a surgical team. I have an MD from Harvard. I am board certified in cardio thoracic medicine and trauma surgery. I have been awarded citations from seven different medical boards in New England. And I am never ever sick at sea.

So I ask you...when someone goes into that chapel and they fall on their knees and they pray to God that their wife doesn't miscarry, or their daughter doesn't bleed to death, or their mother doesn't suffer acute neural trauma from post-operative shock, who do you think they are praying to?

No...go ahead and read your Bible and go to your church and with any luck you might win the annual raffle, but if you are looking for God, he was in Operating Room Number Two on November 17th and he doesn't like to be second-guessed.

You ask me if I have a God Complex? Let me tell you something. I am God!

How do you spot the Rock Star? Are you kidding me? It's about *me* baby! It's about a Feelings DAM taken to the max, man! Want an example? Take Charlie Sheen where he says:

I am on a drug. It's called Charlie Sheen.

A Rock Star is an entitled, righteous, perfectionistic jerk on steroids! Literally! They are on themselves, just as if they were on uppers or on downers, on growth hormones or on steroids, or on all of them at once. What is the difference between the Entitled and the Rock Star? The Rock Star actually gets what they feel they are entitled to. Charlie Sheen also once said this: *I think what drove me insane for a long time is feeling like I hadn't earned most of what I achieved because it came so fast.* Shockingly, a Rock Star, will claim they are the victim. Their behavior isn't their fault, as in what Sheen claims: *As kids we're not taught how to deal with success; we're taught how to deal with failure. If at first you don't succeed, try, try, again. If at first you succeed, then what?*

What! This is the sign of a person who has no significant mission in life—no mission that will challenge them and fulfill their need for significance, contribution, connection, or growth. Sheen thought success was measured by material things like money and it isn't. Sheen says he succeeded, but he didn't. He was blinded by his addiction to feed his feelings DAM.

I had some reservations about going to St. Olaf College because it was a Lutheran school where I would have to take two semesters of religious studies. I was raised Catholic, didn't like going to church that much, and I rarely read the Bible. What I found fascinating was my absolute love of the theological nature of the courses that encouraged inquiry, discussion, and critical thinking.

When I got an A in my Christian Theology class, my dad said half kiddingly, "Son, I think you may have found your calling."

I loved going to chapel service almost every morning. I listened to the sermonizing and listened to the power of the organ and the power of the chapel choir that occasionally mixed with the world famous St. Olaf Choir. So much of the message was about mission; about finding a higher purpose; about never giving up on what your heart tells you is right; about mistakes and redemption; about the Prodigal Son returning home with a humble heart. The message was about the ultimate sacrifice, eternal love, and about the human spirit. There is a reason why sacred beliefs and rituals are at the heart of any culture. Culture is the pursuit of humanity, which is infinitely valuable. The problem with the Rock Star is they trash the thing that makes them most valuable, their humanity. They are completely consumed with selfish pursuits. Like the Prodigal Son returning home, we can only hope they, too, will return. What they choose is out of our control.

Nothing trashes a person's humanity faster than getting what they want. Look at what happened to Tiger Woods. That is why having your entitlement beliefs fulfilled could be your ultimate undoing! If this happens you have achieved Rock Star status. Congratulations.

Even when the Rock Star shows brief signs of self-awareness, don't count on any permanent change. To us mere "trolls," as Sheen would describe any of us, the life of a Rock Star looks horrible. Sheen thinks trolls are too ignorant to understand. Sheen loves his Rock Star life: *I'm just going to hang out with these two smoking hotties and fly privately around the world. It might be lonely up here, but I sure like the view.*

Too many real Rock Stars die prematurely. Their bodies age faster from their bad life style choices that unfortunately, entitled young people try to emulate. According to a study reported by CBS news, *Life as a Rock Star Can Kill You*, the lives of 1,050 American and European music artists were tracked from between 1965 and 2005. The average age of death for the American rock Star was 42 and the average age of death for the British rock star was 35! What Rock Stars want—attention, significance, love, money, sex, drugs, power—is infinite; it cannot be satisfied. Their trajectory is destruction.

If you have a Rock Star as a CEO, your company will be crushed and explode like a supernova. Is it possible to find a CEO in history that parallels the Rock Star behavior of Charlie Sheen? Yes, in fact, there are many to chose from. There is Angelo Mozilo, the former CEO of Countrywide. There is Jeffrey Skilling and Kenneth Lay of Enron. There is Bernard Ebbers of WorldCom. There is Dennis Kozlowski of Tyco; and many others. My favorite, mostly because he was so incredibly arrogant and said such stupid things, just like Sheen, was Joseph Nacchio of Qwest. According to a *Time Magazine* report, *Top 10 Crooked CEOs*, Nacchio was number five. Bernard Madoff and John Rigas were some of the names ahead of him.

I remember paying my US West phone bill, soon to become my Qwest phone bill, when I lived in Mesa, Arizona. I remember reading an article in the Wall Street Journal about Qwest's takeover of US West, and how Joseph Nacchio used fear to motivate the troops. I remember saying to myself, "This guy really sounds like a jerk." And I didn't think my intuition that something wasn't right meant that much about predicting the future of Qwest. I was wrong. This memory sticks in my head because it was the foundation of the rule I use today: Work is social, behaviors lead results, and our behaviors are governed by our thinking. Since I had some friends working for US West I got to see first hand how quickly a Rock Star could damage a company and the good people in it.

When hiring CEOs, boards of directors look at experience and credentials; Nacchio had both. Even today, boards of directors don't care about how results are achieved, and this was true when Qwest picked Nacchio to run the company.

You could not dispute Nacchio's impressive background. He had a Bachelor's Degree in Electrical Engineering from NYU, he had an MBA from NYU, he had a Master's Degree from MIT, and the prestigious Sloan Fellows Program. He joined AT&T fresh out of school and rose through the ranks quickly. After he completed his Masters at MIT, his career took off like a rocket. Shortly, he was VP of its business markets group, then he was head of the long distance business unit, and then he took over the entire consumer long distance division. In his early 40's, he was the youngest head of a major AT&T division. And he got results. He was able to turn the $20 billion long distance division around in a very short period of time.

It's not as if the Rock Star isn't talented nor unable to perform; it's the destructive nature of the Rock Star that boards of directors fail to appreciate or understand. If they did there wouldn't be such a long list of bad CEOs. Boards of directors need to understand that the behavior of the leader always leads results.

What about Nacchio's behavior? He was feared. And he stretched the limits of ethics. One of his last initiatives at AT&T was to mail $100 checks to consumers hoping to lure them from MCI to AT&T. I remember getting one of these checks in the mail and I looked at it strangely and wondered, "Is this for real?" Nacchio felt entitled to the top job at AT&T. When he knew he wasn't going to get it he left for Qwest. The common Rock Star theme is *me* first; *country, company, family, wife, and kids,* last.

According to the regulators who put together the insider trading case against him, he created a culture of fear right from the start at Qwest. Managers resorted to accounting tricks so they wouldn't be fired. Fear-based management will always produce a crisis, because the Rock Star just wants his results—results he is entitled to and results he will get one way or another. The entitlement of the Rock Star CEO shuts down all communication. This destroys trust within the company, with the suppliers, with the customers, and with the general public.

Then came the hostile take over of US West. Nacchio had this to say to US West employees shortly after the takeover: *Because you wear a clown suit doesn't mean you work for the circus. We'll take off the suits and get down to work, then we'll send out the clowns.*

Nacchio immediately fired 11,000 US West workers to demonstrate his absolute control of the company!

In the end, he had to forfeit $52 million in proceeds from his stock sales, pay a $19 million fine, and serve six years in federal prison after being found guilty of 19 counts of insider trading. Nacchio destroyed his company for his personal benefit. And he is trying to sue the lawyers who represented him in his insider trading trial for malpractice. It just never ends for the Rock Star. All hail Caesar!

The amazing thing about Rock Stars is they can come from any level, not just from the top. The problem for many companies is the Rock Star is hard to recognize. Only by going through the DAMs is the Rock Star revealed. And once identified, dealing with or firing a Rock Star isn't easy. Once companies understand how the DAMs stack, they usually see they don't have one Rock Star, but many. Sometimes they find themselves with a whole department of Rock Stars and by the time this happens, the Rock Stars are usually in complete control of the company. This is a very scary realization and it happens more times than it should.

Take the case of a physical therapist in a chiropractor's office. She was hired because she was confident, reliable, took initiative, and worked hard. The chiropractor was thankful he found someone competent. Then things started to happen. The physical therapist took an interest in other areas of the business. She wanted to know everything she could about every other employee. She started ordering people around, using the excuse that she knew what the doctor wanted.

Before long she claimed she was as important to the practice as the doctor. She claimed she knew as much, if not more, than the doctor. She even started taking clients away from the doctor's practice! Even the doctor saw the therapist as indispensable. He couldn't identify what was going on. He began to think perhaps there was something wrong with him.

Only after he understood the attributes of the Rock Star, how it is their mission to get into the tentacles of the business, how the business is all about them, did the doctor begin to understand what he must do.

I had one doctor tell me about his Rock Star problem. He said he thought he had to pay an employee a large salary because he believed that employee was indispensable. One day his employee showed off his new BMW. The doctor, who could only afford a Honda, realized that he was working for his Rock Star employee! He didn't know what the problem was until he started to understand the Thinking DAMs and how they stack.

It isn't that hard to come up with a really quick check. We just need to go back to the definitions of the Thinking DAMs. First, the Ego DAM:

1) Does this person fail to ask for help, which is making things increasingly unproductive?

   Yes? Well check *one* for jerk and the Ego DAM. Moving on. Second, the Learning DAM:

2) Is this person a know-it-all and there is nothing you know that they don't know (even when you know they don't know it)?

Yes? Well check *two* for perfectionist. Keep going? Ok. Third, the My Precious DAM:

3) Does this person want to be in your business, tell you what you should be doing, but will not allow any suggestion or advice and will not volunteer any information about what they are doing or working on?

Yes again? Wow. We might be onto something. Well check *three* for righteous. If you are getting "yes's," how do you feel about those? Being anxious at this point is typical. Fourth is the Trust DAM:

4) Is this person starting to give signs that they don't think things are fair? They wonder if they can trust you because you clearly don't understand their value and importance. Are you beginning to feel they are indispensible? Are you considering giving them more so that they will trust you more?

Yup. Check *four* for the entitled. Finally, the Feelings DAM:

5) Does this person make it clear that they are alone and their feelings are the only thing that matters in this world? They feel misunderstood and insist their behavior isn't their fault? And they absolutely would never, ever consider changing; that everyone else will just have to deal with what they feel they need?

Yes? Are you sure? Well if you are sure, you have a Rock Star. You might want to just skip over to chapter 8. If you are not sure, then you need to pay more attention to what this person is doing at work.

Another sign that you have a Rock Star has to do with point number three above. My dad was extremely good at hiring people and selecting residents for the demanding Thoracic Surgery program at the Minneapolis VA. My dad would never allow anyone into the program or have anyone on his surgical team if he couldn't get to know them. He wanted to know where they went to school, who they knew, why they chose medicine, and he wanted to learn this information within the context of stories; not from some glib answer to an interview question. If you are dealing with a Rock Star it will be very difficult to get to know them, who their friends are, or what they really believe in. You will always detect a wall that is hiding something. Another warning sign of a Rock Star is no network of people they can tap into to ask for help in solving problems. If you hire a Rock Star CEO don't expect them to bring in a team of people to help, because nobody wants to deal with them. Rock Stars are isolated. Their professional network is shallow.

The worst thing you can do with a Rock Star is give him a reward, especially more resources, a promotion, or more say in what your company does.

I knew an engineer who was very good. He saw himself as the engineering god of the company. This engineer would demonstrate time and time again how much smarter he was than anybody else. If you came up with a way to do something and everyone agreed to do it, he would come in and demonstrate the superiority of his way. Because of this, everyone thought he was talented, even a genius. And, as he did this more and more, people in the company began to see him as indispensible. Then he got a promotion. He had his own assistants, and ran a significant section of the plant.

He worked in almost total isolation. He controlled who could have daily communication with him. He expected the company to serve him, if anything got in his way he quickly became outraged.

This engineer handled a number of important projects for one of the company's largest customers. He refused to communicate with others who needed to know what he was doing and started controlling the conversations with this customer.

For a while the customer put up with this because he also thought this Rock Star was indispensable. But as time went by, the Rock Star's behavior deteriorated further and he became ruder, terser and more arrogant. A monster of the worst kind was beginning to hatch.

More and more of what he was working on became invisible. Supplies and materials began to disappear because he wouldn't follow proper procedures for signing things out. As a result, there would be unexpected interruptions in production and the company began falling behind on its deliveries. Other customers started to complain. Parts shortages grew. Nobody really knew what this Rock Star engineer was doing and he wasn't talking.

So a new policy was introduced. All engineers would work within a SCRUM, a special project team that brought the customer together with the engineering, sales, and service teams to serve a common objective. The SCRUM required the team to communicate every day and report what each member did and what they were going to do next. All of the work was catalogued.

This required 100% transparency and the Rock Star slowly refused to comply with the process. He refused to report his work and refused to communicate or work with the team. And he thought he could get away with it.

When important customer projects fell behind, prototype builds failed in the field, and nobody knew or understood what he was doing, the Rock Star had to be fired. Finally, when the team leader really pressed for information, the Rock Star became completely insubordinate and was promptly escorted out of the building.

He couldn't believe he had been fired. He said that the CEO would not tolerate his dismissal. The team leader told him that the

CEO already agreed with the decision that had been made several days before. With tears in his eyes, the Rock Star realized that his kingdom was no more. He had been removed and he could never return. *"Et tu, Brute?"*

Gaius Aurelius Valerius Diocletianus Augustus, or for short Diocletian, who ruled in the fourth century A.D. was the last non-Christian emperor of the Roman Empire. He was born in Dalmatia, the coastal region of the former Yugoslavia and known as Croatia today. When he came to power, the Roman Empire was in trouble. Independent states were feuding and centralized authority was weakening. Diocletian was smart enough to figure out a way to delegate the management of the Empire. He created three more divine leaders, or Caesars, each of whom ruled a quarter of the empire. By doing this, he was able to unify the empire for another 300 years.

In the first century B.C., as Rome was becoming an empire, slavery increased exponentially. In the Italian Peninsula alone there were reported to be two to three million slaves, a little less than half of the population. Slave life was harsh and there were many revolts, the most famous led by the gladiator Spartacus. It was a massive uprising that shook Roman leadership to its core. Spartacus and his roughly 120,000 followers attempted to flee the country. They failed and were all brutally killed. At the time, it seemed impossible that the Roman Empire would change so that all of its people could be free.

Then Christianity entered the picture. Christianity placed Caesar second to God.

Diocletian would have none of it. He would not be placed second to a Christian God. He was the one and only God! He made it clear that all Roman citizens were to worship him, and him alone, and he had unlimited power. He had the power to decide who was a slave and who was free, who would live and who would die. He would not tolerate insubordination. He refused to have anything less than absolute control of the empire. And he was enraged when Christians would not abandon faith in their God. Seeing this as a threat to his absolute power to control everything in the empire, Diocletian ordered all Christians killed. This was known in history as Diocletian's *Great Persecution*. It failed.

More and more of the population converted to Christianity. Christians valued the reward of the afterlife and saw their death as freedom and a gateway to heaven. Where Spartacus failed, Christianity created an exit ramp out of slavery and persecution and into the kingdom of Heaven. In his quest for power, Diocletian failed to understand what he was dealing with. As a result of his need to be ruthless and create fear, life for the Romans was intolerable and it was impossible to be happy. With more misery for more people came more people that wanted to escape. Seeing martyrs willing to die in a joyful way and hearing the Christian stories of a wonderful afterlife, Christianity became the escape from the hell being generated from Diocletian. More than any other Caesar of Rome, Diocletian created the greatest growth rate of Christianity. He failed miserably in his objective, even though his solution appeared to be logical and correct.

After Diocletian abdicated in A.D. 313, the persecution ended. Under his successor, Constantine, Rome eventually adopted Christianity as its religion.

Diocletian returned to his home to build a huge palace on the blood, sweat, and tears of his Christian slaves. He thought he would own his palace forever; that it would always represent his divinity; that countless generations would be awed by the symbol of his greatness. The palace quickly became a treasured symbol to the Catholic Church because it represented the man who inspired so many to convert to Christianity. By keeping it a holy place that tells and retells the stories of what happened, the palace continues to inspire millions of Christians and will likely continue for many generations to come.

The Roman Emperor who set out to destroy Christianity succeeded in building a country that is now considered one of the strongest footholds of Catholicism. Croatia has been visited by the Pope more times than almost any other country, and has one of the holiest Christian monuments—the grand Diocletian's Palace! *"Et tu, Brute?"*

If you don't want to wind up like Diocletian, there are some great CEOs that we can model. There is Steve Jobs, Mary Kay Ash, Tim Brown of IDEO, Tony Hsieh of Zappos, Akio Morita the former CEO of Sony, Harold Geneen the former CEO of ITT, Lee Iacocca the former CEO of Chrysler, Andrew Carnegie the former CEO of US Steel, Ray Kroc the former CEO of McDonalds, Earl Bakken the former CEO of Medtronic, Bill George the former CEO of Medtronic, Tomas Watson Jr. the former CEO of IBM, Louis V. Gerstner Jr. the former CEO of IBM, Erwin Kelm the former CEO of Cargill.

I carefully picked these names. It wasn't about some fancy survey where the data is over analyzed and thought to death. The criteria was simple. First, they had to have a story you could read about in a book or books. Second, they had to overcome some impossible challenge, which was personal to them. Third, the story had to show how they defined their success and how they realized their success in a way that was transformative—they became better people, which in turn made their people better, which resulted in a better company. Fourth, it had to be a story about serving people rather than taking from people. Work is social, behaviors lead results, and our behaviors are governed by our thinking.

I started this chapter with a fictitious Rock Star surgeon who thought he was God. Let me end this story about a real surgeon who had a huge impact on the world. The greatest heart transplant surgeon in the world was Norman Shumway. Dr. Christiaan Barnard is more famous, because he was the first. But without Norm's careful scientific research and working out procedurally how it should be done, Barnard would have failed. Barnard wanted fame and got it. Norm wanted to make heart transplantation work and dedicated his life humbly to that mission. Barnard and Shumway took two very different trajectories in their lives. This is exactly the danger you face when hiring a CEO. Did you select the guy who wants to be famous, to be a Rock Star? Or did you select the gal who wants to make your company and the people in it something special, something different, something great? You need to know, because the trajectories and outcomes are dramatically different depending on the type of leader selected.

Norm was a very close and beloved friend of my father. The impact he had on my dad and his life was huge. And it was through my dad's stories about him that I learned to stand up for what is right; I learned to stand up for my own personal mission. I learned to have a sense of humor and not take myself too seriously. No dad tells stories about a Rock Star CEO to inspire their children to be great! And even if he did there isn't much to tell, other than, "Once upon a time there was a Rock Star who lived on a hill, who had everything he wanted, did everything for himself, and then died."

Shumway was loved by his patients, loved by the doctors he trained, and loved by the surgical teams he led. How many retired CEOs can say that about themselves? From his obituary,

'I never worked so hard in my life and never learned so much and had so much responsibility at a young age,' said William Brody, M.D., Ph.D., president of John Hopkins University and a Shumway trainee. 'He was a brilliant teacher and a master psychologist. With his humor, he always made it fun. To be in

the operating room with Shumway was the height of your day because he was brilliant and witty. At a time when everybody made cardiac surgery seem complex, he made it seem easy.'

Did Norm Shumway drive a fancy car, a Bentley, a Rolls, a Mercedes, or a BMW? No, he typically drove a beat up, run down car because he simply didn't care. In fact, he would step out of the lime light and encourage the doctors he trained to develop fast so that they could have careers that exceeded his own. There was no *My Precious DAM* with Norm Shumway. It's no wonder that he worked on the thing that made him so special to the world—the human heart. I had a prominent executive tell me once, "Gray, I always can find and hire someone with the skills. But it is a long and hard search to find someone that has it in their heart to want to be a great human being."

So few CEOs in the United States today have a heart as large as Norm Shumway. If they did our products would lead the world and our companies would provide meaningful jobs to so many.

CHAPTER 5 SUMMARY

Chapter 5 is about the God Complex, which is created when all of the Thinking DAMs are active and interacting. It is a Feelings DAM on top of the entitled, righteous, perfectionist jerk. Another name for a person with a God Complex in this book is Rock Star. To the Rock Star, everything is about him. Yes, he may be talented. Yes, she may be a good worker. And even if they are not, they will make you believe they are. But when you start to believe they are indispensable, you have fallen for their trap. Rock Stars control. If he is your employee, you will start to work for him. If he is the CEO, you will lose everything that was good about your company. The earlier you identify your Rock Star the better. The worst thing you can do is to promote a Rock Star. The worst mistake you can make is to think you can rehabilitate the Rock Star.

The Rock Star, with his horrible behavior, is not a new phenomenon. Rock Stars have been with us since the dawn of civilization. Diocletian hailed from a long line of Roman emperors who were self-serving at best. Today we see this behavior from movie stars to sports stars to actual rock n' roll stars, and, sadly, with way too many CEOs. The common denominator is a worship of self. And as a result they fail to leave a meaningful impact on the world or a legacy for others to model and learn from. Instead of assassination, as in the time of Rome, choose to we just let the Rock Star flame out.

Young people who want to succeed in business need to understand the true pursuit of mission that exists outside of themselves, which serves a universal and in a way a spiritual purpose. They need to emulate people like Steve Jobs and Norman Shumway.

ARE YOU A ROCK STAR?

Instructions: Find a partner. If you can do that, it probably means you're not a Rock Star! Or they are not a partner, they are a slave and they are going to do anything you ask. Answer the questions and use your partner as a coach so that both of you agree. Good luck.

Record your answers and ask one other (honest) person to record their answers as well.

1= Never 2= Seldom 3= Sometimes 4= Usually 5= Always

➤ Do you feel the company serves you and only you? To hell with customers, employees, bosses, investors, or the board.

1   2   3   4   5

➤ Are you verbally abusive to people and want them to fear you?

1   2   3   4   5

➤ Do you think you can get away with anything?

1   2   3   4   5

➤ Do you fire people as soon as they fail you?

1   2   3   4   5

➤ Do things come easy for you and feel that success is just a given?

1   2   3   4   5

➤ Do you boast about your work performance?

1   2   3   4   5

➤ Do you think you are the most important person in the company?

1   2   3   4   5

➤ Is it impossible to have too much and be paid too much?

1   2   3   4   5

➤ Do you demand total obedience?

1   2   3   4   5

➤ Is it impossible to climb the corporate ladder and experience success too fast?

1   2   3   4   5

19 or below

You are in good shape. You aren't trying to control the world and that is a good thing. You don't let your feelings get out of control and you stay level-headed. Stay on track, ask yourself what areas in previous chapters you scored high on and which ones you need to work on. If you scored a 20 or below in every chapter, and this is an honest representation of your behaviors and how you think, congratulations, you are a flow thinker and an asset to any company!

20 to 39

You have many of the elements associated with a God Complex. You need to realize that this is going to be a show stopper for you. If you get promoted and are given more power, it just isn't going to be enough for you. You need to understand how other people contribute. You need to understand what a company really represents and how it works. You really need to understand ethics and social responsibility! You have to start seeing what you are doing as only one role that needs to be played in order for the entire company to function. The reality is, you are not the most important person in the company. You can easily be replaced. You serve a role. A role where people count on you and you must help them as they help you. Most importantly, you need to ask the help of a trusted friend who can guide you to become a better person.

40 or above

This isn't good. I am really wondering why you are reading this book. And I can't believe you scored yourself so high. If this score really reflects the true you, I have nothing to offer or say to you. You are a God. You know everything. I am nothing more than a troll. Forgive me.

DO YOU WORK WITH ROCK STARS?

Instructions: Find a partner. Describe the people you work closely with, what your boss is like, what the leadership is like. Take your time with the stories and include details because often the little things matter as much as the big things. Read the questions below and try to come up with answers that represent the truth as best you can. Good luck.

Record your answers and ask one other (honest) person to record their answers as well.

1= Never 2= Seldom 3= Sometimes 4= Usually 5= Always

➤ Do most people who work for the company seem incredibly frustrated and to some degree suffering emotional pain?

                                           1   2   3   4   5

➤ Are some of the leaders in the company verbally abusive and is everyone afraid of them?

    1   2   3   4   5

➤ Do some people think the rules don't apply to them and that they can get away with anything?

    1   2   3   4   5

➤ Do company leaders fire people suddenly in the company with no explanation or process?

    1   2   3   4   5

➤ Are there some leaders (golden boys) in the company who just seem to have a meteoric rise, with no explanation of what they actually accomplished for the company?

    1   2   3   4   5

➤ Do some managers and leaders continually boast about their work performance and really not care what you are doing?

    1   2   3   4   5

➤ Do some people in your company think it wouldn't survive without them?

    1   2   3   4   5

➤ Are some managers and leaders paid outrageous sums of money and yet try to pursue even more as if they can't be satisfied?

    1   2   3   4   5

➤ Is everyone too afraid to confront the Rock Star and his bad behavior and so that it looks like he will never ever be removed?

    1   2   3   4   5

> ➤ Can you imagine your company being several times better just by the removal of a single person and his bad Rock Star behavior?

1   2   3   4   5

19 or below

You work for a good company! Did your company score low on many of the others chapters? If a company isn't monitoring their behaviors they likely have at least one person in one key position that is making a huge percentage of the work population unhappy. If a company doesn't have a single Rock Star, then it's likely the work culture is deliberately managed to prevent this. That is why I can't recommend strongly enough Robert Sutton's book, *The No Asshole Rule*.

20 to 39

Well this is probably 90% of companies. Most companies have at least one Rock Star in a key position. In order to neutralize the Rock Star in a company, align yourself with others on significant initiatives so that the Rock Star can't interfere with what you are doing. The best way is to get alignment with customers. This will work even if the Rock Star is a CEO. But if the Rock Star is really insecure, this will only work for a while. As long as things are going well, you are safe. But if you do something that makes him feel he isn't in control, and things start going downhill for the company, well, get ready to be fired. So always keep a look out for better companies to work for.

40 or above

This is sad. Why do smart people work for a company with so many Rock Stars? Money. It seems, especially with startup companies where a lot of money is thrown around, the money attracts the worst people; people who boast about their own self-importance, who feel incredibly entitled, and who are Rock Stars. In order to keep others working at such a miserable company, the Rock Stars either give the employees a lot of money (rare) or they give the illusion that employees will get a lot of money through stock options or bonus programs (most common). Anytime you feel you have to work for a company just because of the money is when you will find your life and soul being sucked out of you. You need to shut your eyes, call a head-hunter, and get out of there now.

CHAPTER 6

The Victim is a Tar Baby! Stay Away!

Evil requires the sanction of the victim.

—Ayn Rand

The Rock Star cannot exist without a victim. The intent of the Rock Star is power over others—to tell them what to do, what to think, and in general, to direct their lives. The Rock Star doesn't want anyone around them who challenges or makes them feel weak. What they want are loyal lieutenants: people who sacrifice their freedom to contribute their own ideas just so they don't get fired. If you are working for a Rock Star or have a Rock Star as your subordinate, then you, my friend, may be their victim.

Nothing is ever the victim's fault. Ever. All of their problems are caused by others—usually the Rock Star, and there is absolutely nothing they can do about it. (Strangely, all Rock Stars are also victims too! Their problems are the fault of the incompetent trolls who repeatedly fail them.)

The currency for victims is compassion. They want you to feel sorry for them. They want you to listen to their hopeless plight. Soon enough, they will likely probe you to see if you are willing to sacrifice your own life and happiness to rescue them. There is no motive for the victim to actually change. In fact, like flesh-eating zombies, if you try to rescue them, they will try to make you a victim, too. Misery loves company!

The victim has all of the thinking DAMs, just like the Rock Star. They have the ego DAM, where they don't ask for help. They have the Learning DAM, where there is nothing new to discover. They have the My Precious DAM, where they aggressively protect their wretched situation. They have the Trust DAM, where they feel you and others are out to get them. They have the Feelings DAM, because they have no purpose other than getting as many people to feel sorry for them as possible. Why does the victim have all of these DAMs? Because, the victim doesn't want to take any responsibility for changing their circumstances. In other words, the victim is a tar baby.

To refresh your memory, Tar-Baby is a fictional character appearing in the second of the Uncle Remus stories, published in 1881. The Tar Baby, a doll made of tar and turpentine, was used by Br'er Fox to entrap Br'er Rabbit. As Br'er Rabbit tries to separate from the Tar Baby the more entangled he becomes. A victim does the same thing. They will use your natural, altruistic instinct against you.

The language of the victim is as deadly as the Sirens in Homer's Odyssey. Listening to their song, your desire to rescue them will grow. However, attempting to rescue them will leave you with no one in control of your life. And with no one in control, just like the ships described in the Odyssey, you are destined to crash into the rocks and meet your demise. Yes, for your own good, stay a safe distance away from the Sirens! Do not accept or buy into the sweet helplessness of their song, no matter what! Like Odysseus ordered his men to do aboard their ship, plug your ears with beeswax until you are a safe distance away, or better, put on earphones and listen to Tony Robbins monologues, if you must.

Hitler's rise to power was enabled by the world economic collapse of 1929. Most of the population felt helpless. Looking for any solution out of their trouble, the German people bought into Hitler's song. They gave their freedom, their power, and their souls to Hitler, who saw himself as the Fatherland's great rescuer. And the German people identified with Hitler; they even sympathized with him, because he was a victim just like them! They listened to Hitler and his deadly song, the one that painted Germany as a victim of the Jews. As a result, millions of Jews and other groups lost their lives, their families and for a time, their cultures. All of Germany was destroyed.

Jews and others keep the memory of the Holocaust alive, as they should—for the sake of all humankind. But Jews don't do it from the mindset of a victim. The state of Israel, with its robust military, is evidence of that! When Saddam Hussein launched SCUD missiles in the first Gulf War, Israel made it clear to Norman Schwarzkopf that if he didn't destroy all of the SCUDs immediately, Israel would, with everything they had. Israel would not be a victim! This became Norman Schwarzkopf's top priority. He knew Israel meant business.

When confronted with the Rock Star, we can choose to take action against them or we can choose to be the victim. Rabbi Jonathan Sacks explains our choice brilliantly...

Something bad happens. There are two responses. Number one we can complain. Number two we can do something about it. Now…if we simply complain. If we see ourselves as victims. The truth is that there is good news with being the victim. Everyone has compassion for you. Everyone has rachmones for you. It is comfortable being the victim. The only trouble with being a victim is by defining yourself as such you have put yourself out of any possible way of improving your situation. Because if it isn't your fault you can't put it right. Somebody else has to. And you thereby hand over your life to somebody else. The Jewish way is to say if I see something wrong in the world let me be one of the first to put it right. That is responsibility. And that literally is what responsibility means. God is calling to us as he called to the first human being in the Garden of Eden. Yahweh where are you? Help me put out the fire. And that is the Jewish way not to see ourselves as victims even though we have been victims. But to see ourselves as responsible agents who working together in conjunction with one another and with that little voice from heaven, can change the world. That is the only way to be.

What Jonathan says here is extremely useful, because it provides us with a metric in our own company. For example, if you want to know whether you have a Rock Star who is persecuting or bullying people in your company, look to see who's complaining, how many are complaining, and what are they complaining about. A leader in a business has two choices with complaining: he can ignore and suppress the complaints and pretend they don't exist or he can investigate the complaints and see what is at the source. If the leader chooses to ignore the complaints the reason may be that it's because the problem points to him as the source. For example, he may be a Rock Star or he may be comfortable playing the role of victim to the Rock Star. In this case, efforts are made to suppress those who are complaining, through intimidation or removal, through reassignments or firing. Or, he may simply state his hands are tied due to circumstances out of his control. The net effect of ignoring or not addressing the problem is to not take responsibility for the problem. And that is called being a victim. This action creates a population of victims who render their situation hopeless. A key sign that this has happened is when requests are made, nothing gets done; the excuse is, "It is not my job."

The other choice is to collect the complaints and study the pattern and decide what they mean, thereby fixing the business and putting it on a powerful path for growth. Doing this prevents the dreadful victim—prosecutor—rescuer drama triangle (which we will get to in a moment). In order to break the triangle, this almost always requires the immediate removal or expulsion of the Rock Star, which can only happen if the victim decides he or she wants to be free of the Rock Star's reign. It doesn't matter if it's a dentist with a Rock Star hygienist, a CEO with a Rock Star plant manager, or a woman wanting to divorce her Rock Star husband, in every case that I have experienced, when the Rock Star is removed, everyone else rises to meet the challenge provided they are encouraged to do so. This creates a great outpouring of productivity fueled by the emotion of the people who have suffered. It's one of the greatest gifts a business leader can provide to their employees. But in order for this to happen, it requires the strength of at least one victim to rise up.

The victim must rise up to be the Maverick or the Iconoclast—he or she must take the independent action to be the first to make a stand—to take bold and sudden action to break the bonds and not take orders from the tyrant for one more day. This may mean direct challenge, out right insubordination, or even organizing a mutiny of an entire department. The victim must do this in order to win back their right to enjoy life, liberty, and the pursuit of happiness that Thomas Jefferson wrote about in our Declaration of Independence. Nobody should ever feel like their freedom is limited or that they are a slave.

To make the choice to take a stand is not an easy thing to do. It requires completely breaking free of the feelings DAM. It means it might cost you your job. It means that your comfortable life working in the dysfunctional culture is gone. But it will build your self-esteem, because you will be seen as a person with strength and integrity. By not being the victim anymore, you will have earned the respect of good people and show true leadership by example. You will be remembered. People will tell stories about you. You will have provided a meaning to your life. You might even ascend to hero status in the eyes of others. All of this doesn't make it any easier.

There is a field of psychology and psychotherapy called transactional analysis (TA). One of the popular archetypes or constructs is called the *drama triangle*. There are three roles to be played: the persecutor, the victim, and the rescuer. Each of the actors in the triangle gets a payoff, or reward from the other two. For example, the victim receives a reward from the rescuer in the form of sympathy and attention. The victim gets a reward from the persecutor's grievous interactions that provide ample justification for getting even more attention and sympathy. The persecutor's reward is the satisfaction of having complete control of the victim. Finally, the rescuer is rewarded with the fulfillment of feeling needed—that the victim couldn't survive without him. The result of this complex dance is that nothing gets done, no problem is solved, and everyone is trapped.

According to the theory, the only way to break the drama triangle is by stopping the payoffs that each role is receiving. For the victim this means showing the persecutor that she is no longer in control of him as well as showing the rescuer that he will take full responsibility for his situation and no longer needs to be rescued. The former victim may ask for help, but he owns the problem and challenge and will get the self-satisfaction of changing his life for the better.

Let me give you an example. It's easy for me or any consultant to fall into the role of rescuer. In fact there are many people who expect that is what a consultant is suppose to do, but it never is. In a way, being the rescuer consultant could be very profitable, but also immoral and degrading since what you are doing will never help the client.

I have a good friend who is a consultant. He had a client who was a very large division of a monstrously large corporate conglomerate. A year prior he had conducted a very detailed customer satisfaction survey and the score wasn't very good. He noticed then that the person calling the shots, the general manager for the business, an ex-professional athlete, was a Rock Star. The Rock Star challenged everything my friend presented. The GM was rude to his direct reports. His typical response was that if in fact there was a problem, which he doubted, he would fix it. So that seemed to be the end of it. The GM didn't think much of my friend's effort.

The next year, my friend was asked again to put together another detailed survey of their customers. By this time, things had gotten significantly worse. As he completed his work, others on the Rock Star's management team secretly told my friend that he needed to save them. He needed to rescue them from their tyrannical boss. In the meeting he should stand up against the Rock Star and put him in his place! My friend asked me what he should do. I think he did this more as a double check of his own thinking, because he is really good at this kind of stuff.

The problem was that the people who reported to the Rock Star were just as responsible for the poor performance of the business because they were behaving like victims. As you will see in the next chapter, the solution to any problem your business has is never outside the four walls of your company. It is always within your four walls. For example, the leadership team could try to get the Rock Star to agree that certain behaviors are damaging to the business and should not be accepted within the team. In this way they could collectively police the new policy.

Here is another example. Knowing that the GM needs to have control, they could defy his wishes subversively. For example, on a decision the Rock Star made that is blatantly wrong, they could collectively do what was right for the business instead of what he wanted. When the GM finally gets wise that he isn't getting what he wants and insists on finding the person (or incompetent troll) who is responsible, they could send him off on a very lengthy and complicated trail of investigation of "who done it." The possibilities for frustrating the Rock Star are boundless.

I worked with a client who had a Rock Star plant manager who reported to the General Manager. He wanted me to somehow rehabilitate the plant manager. Once it was clear to me in one meeting that he was in fact a Rock Star and needed to be fired, the GM thought I was crazy to bring up this idea. And since the GM would be overseas working hard to establish a new plant and a new market the idea of firing the plant manager would be unthinkable, because it would dangerously destabilize the business. The GM started to explore what the plant manager was open to, and what he found out was the plant manager wasn't open to much. What he found was a bunch of DAM thinking. For example, the plant manager didn't feel the business needed to grow, that the people beneath him needed to be weak, and that he liked to make his boss look weak. For example, he said, "This is what my boss said wrong; let me correct him now," in an important customer meeting. It became increasingly clear to the GM that the plant manager was a Rock Star and needed to be fired. But he couldn't pull the trigger. The key to remember is that the Rock Star is only powerful if you agree to be their victim.

What this general manager was hoping for that would get him out of his predicament was to be rescued. He was hoping that employees or customers of the business would call the owner and complain and the owner would want him fired or the plant manager would get in a fight with the owner and the owner would fire him on the spot. Yes he hoped somehow to be rescued, but he also realized this would likely never happen and this strangely was comforting to him. Even though the situation was bad, nothing was going to change. Even when a situation is bad, it is *the devil we know*. The unknown scares us sometimes to our very bones.

In McDowell Mountain Park just northeast of Phoenix, close to where I live, there is a series of mountain-bike loops. One of these loops is called the technical loop. I have ridden this loop often with my friend Colonel Carl Schott, US Army, whom I talk about in *Change Your DAM Thinking*. He was the one that explained to me about the importance of planning and how *the very best plan never survives the first bullet*. Within the first mile of this loop, there is a descent down a cliff face. It is a harrowing jump, which I always refused to do. Often, the Colonel would shout at me, telling me I didn't deserve to be a man, did I need my mommy to hold my hand, stuff like that. I knew what he was doing, so I wasn't offended. What I was facing is what Bob Proctor, the famous motivational guru, would call the Terror Barrier. The new idea, called "Y," was to go over the cliff on the bike. The old idea, called "X," was for me to avoid this and walk down the steps on the right. Every time I got to the top of the cliff with my bike, with the colonel shouting at me from the bottom, I was conflicted. I felt extremely confused and anxious. I wanted to do it, but I didn't want to break my neck either. The fact that the Colonel had broken his back and some ribs on a mountain bike ride once and ridden back to the house in pain didn't help matters.

In theory, in order to cross the terror barrier and do the "Y," you have to teach yourself as much as possible about the "Y". In this case, there wasn't much to learn. What I did know is the Colonel was able to do it, but I questioned his sanity. However, one day, a girl on a mountain bike said hello to me and quickly descended down the cliff face. I know what you are thinking. If a girl can do it so could I and you are exactly right! But I had recorded what she did in my mind's eye like a slow-motion movie, frame by frame. I saw how she was positioned on the bike, how she was braking, the speed she entered the descent, the line she choose down the descent, and how she accelerated freely and gracefully down to the bottom. I said, "Ok, I can do this." So I pedaled my bike back away from the cliff, turned my bike around to face my enemy, and proceeded forward. The moment I started to descend the cliff I was terrified; I think I shut my eyes for a moment and wondered if I was going to die. Somehow, I forced my body to relax and let gravity take over, and I did it. When I got to the bottom, I shot a look to the Colonel that basically said, "Don't you dare say anything!" I was thrilled that I had done it.

The terror barrier never goes away and you never get use to it. As you experience these kinds of growth breakthroughs you notice the feelings and anxiety as a welcome friend. You say to yourself, "Ok, I know what this is. This is the Terror Barrier. Here we go again." In chapter 10, you will read about how I stood up for what is right and told an important, potential customer, in no uncertain terms, that I would not guarantee them what they wanted. Because of my honesty and integrity, we won the contract. But, in that moment of truth, I never felt more alone, more vulnerable, and more terrified. It was exactly the same feeling I felt when I started to descend over the cliff face, wondering if I was going to live. Change is never comfortable. It won't make you comfortable. It will not make your employees comfortable. It will not make your boss comfortable. If you want to stop being the victim then the price you must be willing to pay is the price of discomfort, of stretching yourself emotionally to your limits, and breaking through your own terror barrier. Only you can do this. Nobody else. Your reward will be your freedom.

CHAPTER 6 SUMMARY

The Rock Star only has power if she has a victim. The victim abdicates his power to the Rock Star. It is a choice the victim freely makes. The victim looks for someone from the outside to rescue them. This is known in transactional analysis as the *drama triangle* where the persecutor, victim, and rescuer have specific roles and currency. The victim can only break free of the bonds of the drama triangle by deciding that she will no longer be the victim. She needs to tell the Rock Star, the persecutor, that he has no power over her anymore. She needs to tell the rescuer that she is going to take responsibility for her own situation and through her own work make things better. As easy as this is to say in theory, in real life it is a very difficult thing for any victim to do. By standing up to the Rock Star you could lose your promotion or your job. But you will be free and you will have strengthened your self-esteem and earned the respect of others. Your life will no longer be dammed up by DAM thinking. Your life will have purpose. But this doesn't mean that if it happens again and you find yourself being a victim again that it will be any easier or any less terrifying for you to break free. It will always be terrifying to embrace change and an uncertain future.

ARE YOU A VICTIM?

Instructions: Find a partner. Do not order them around and tell them they have to help you, or else! Or else what? What are you going to do to them? If they buy into your nonsense and need for absolute control then they aren't a partner or friend who can help you. They are your slave. And as they read this book with you, they will break free! Anyway, try to follow these instructions. And I just want you to know I am not ordering you to do anything. You are free to do what you choose.

Record your answers and ask another (honest and free) person to record his answers as well.

1 = Never 2 = Seldom 3 = sometimes 4 = Usually 5 = Always

➤ Does a Rock Star run your life?

1 2 3 4 5

➤ Do you complain about the Rock Star almost out of habit?

1 2 3 4 5

➤ Do you get mad at others for not being able to rescue you?

1 2 3 4 5

➤ Do you enjoy the sympathy from others because of your victimization?

1 2 3 4 5

➤ Are you always rejecting advice from others on how you can make your situation better?

1 2 3 4 5

➤ Do you tell others that offer advice that they don't understand you?

1 2 3 4 5

➤ Is your identity strongly attached to you being a victim?

1 2 3 4 5

> Do you say, "It's not my job" at work?

$$1 \quad 2 \quad 3 \quad 4 \quad 5$$

> Does taking action against the Rock Star seem utterly impossible to you?

$$1 \quad 2 \quad 3 \quad 4 \quad 5$$

> Do you disagree with my notion about the Feelings DAM blocking purpose?

$$1 \quad 2 \quad 3 \quad 4 \quad 5$$

19 or below

Look up to the stars and thank God you are free.

20 to 39

Ok. You are a victim. You need to learn about the drama triangle, learn about the terror barrier, talk to people who have broken free of their victim roles, and ask for help and advice from others. Then look at your life. Write down what your life could be like without being a victim and having the Rock Star persecute you. Then write down why cutting yourself free of victimhood scares you. Remember, when you are a victim you have no power. When you are no longer bound by victimhood, you are truly free.

40 or Above

You really are a victim. So what do you want to do about it? Don't look to me to rescue you. If you start complaining I will put my headphones on. Don't be surprised if I don't want to get within ten feet of you.

IS YOUR COMPANY FULL OF VICTIMS?

Instructions: Find a partner. Do not order him around and tell him they must help you or else! If your partner doesn't work for your company, tell him a story that supports your position and let him ask you questions and probe, and then let him come up with his own score.

Record your answers and ask another (honest and free) person to record his answers as well.

1 = Never 2 = Seldom 3 = sometimes 4 = Usually 5 = Always

➢ Does a Rock Star run the lives of others in the company?

| 1 | 2 | 3 | 4 | 5 |

➢ Do people complain about the Rock Star(s) almost out of habit?

| 1 | 2 | 3 | 4 | 5 |

➢ Do people in your company get mad at you or others because you won't rescue them, possibly even calling you names?

| 1 | 2 | 3 | 4 | 5 |

➢ Would you say people in your company enjoy the identity of being the victim?

| 1 | 2 | 3 | 4 | 5 |

➢ Are people in your company always rejecting your advice on how they could be free from being the victim?

| 1 | 2 | 3 | 4 | 5 |

➢ Do others in your company tell you that you couldn't possible understand their situation?

| 1 | 2 | 3 | 4 | 5 |

➢ Do people in your company enjoy their identity as victims?

| 1 | 2 | 3 | 4 | 5 |

➢ Do people in your company say, "It's not my job" at work?

| 1 | 2 | 3 | 4 | 5 |

➤ Do people think taking action against the Rock Star is impossible?

1   2   3   4   5

➤ Do people think I am heartless and selfish because of my description of the Feelings DAM?

1   2   3   4   5

19 or below

Wow. What a wonderful company! I want to come visit!

20 to 39

Ok. You have victim mentality all over. You can try to find a group of people in your company and start figuring out ways to keep the Rock Star on edge without getting fired. You also need to investigate if your company understands how important the behaviors of its leaders are to future business results. If it looks like a change isn't likely, you should contemplate getting out of there, because if you hang around victims too long you will become a victim, too.

40 or Above

Ok. Here is what to do. Figure out a job where you don't have to have much contact with anyone in the company. A field sales job for example. Next, go buy a pair of headphones and always have them in your ears when you are with someone from work. Do not listen to them. Do not listen to them. Did I Mention, DO NOT LISTEN TO THEM?

CHAPTER 7

The Solution Exists Within Your Four Walls

The dogmas of the quiet past are inadequate to the stormy present. The occasion is piled high with difficulty, and we must rise with the occasion. As our case is new, so we must think anew and act anew.

—Abraham Lincoln

After writing the book *Change Your DAM Thinking* and many drafts of this book, many people ask me to tell them the answer. I have to pause and think, because I thought I just told them the answer. It starts with the title on the cover of the first book, *Change Your DAM Thinking*. What caused me to write the second book was this: Most people saw the thinking DAMs in others, but didn't see them in themselves. So I am writing this book, *You Have a DAM Problem*, to show you we all have DAM thinking going on and it is this thinking that prevents us from finding the solutions to our problems. I have a mantra I repeat again and again: *The solution exists within your four walls.* In the decades I have worked on highly technical engineering problems and very complex business problems I have always found this mantra to be true. What defines the four walls? First, there are the four walls of your head. If you are stuck, you need to change your thinking. The solution exists within your four walls. Second, if your family is stuck or in a crisis that they just can't get over, the entire family needs to change their thinking. The solution exists within your four walls. If your business is stuck and just can't grow, the entire company needs to change their thinking. The solution exists within your four walls. Do you have a DAM problem? Change your DAM thinking.

The problem with my solution is that people don't want to give up the way they think. They want a different answer. Sort of like if you want to lose weight, they want an answer where they can still be a coach potato. For example, let's say you come up to me and demand, "I want to lose weight. Tell me the answer on how I can lose weight. I know what my problem is. I am eating too much" And I say to you, "You're right; you are eating too much. It's obvious. So let's just skip to the answer. For your BMI (body mass index) you need to be on a diet of 1500 calories a day (let's say). So you need to follow strictly eating the following meals that amounts to 1000 calories per day." That is an answer. It is a good technical answer. And most of the time for any of us that are over weight it will fail. Sure there may be a success at first, but it won't be sustainable. Why? You have been given an answer that is outside of your four walls.

Anytime I work with a client on a technical problem or a business problem, I work hard to get within their four walls. I have to see the world the way they are seeing it. Why? Because the real solution is within their four walls. What I am saying isn't anything new. It is what a good therapist , or psychologist, or psychiatrist does. They get into their clients four walls. Over eating is a psychological problem. It requires work to solve it. Work is social. It takes a behavioral change to adopt a different pattern of living. Behaviors lead results. In order to change the behavior it requires a change in thinking. Behaviors are governed by our thinking. The same is true for any complex business problem. It's psychological. It is sociological. It demands different thinking in order to generate different patterns of behavior, which in turn defines a new company culture. A new culture is key to transforming a stuck business into a growing business.

How should you start in your search for a solution? Look inside yourself first and make sure your thinking is right: no Ego, no Learning, no My Precious, no Trust, and no Feelings DAMs. That means people will be attracted to you, because you are not a Rock Star, that is an entitled, perfectionist, righteous, jerk. The solution demands that you have the ability to attract others to help you, where you trust them to get into your four walls. It's the only way.

If you are stuck on a complex business problem right now, and you think you don't have any of these thinking DAMs, you're wrong. If you think you can solve this problem without changing your thinking, you're wrong. If you think you can solve this problem without finding and attracting the help you need, you're wrong.

If you don't believe me, here is what you need to do. Invite a non-exempt employee to your office. Make a random choice, meaning pick a name out of a hat where the selection is blind (yes I am serious). When they come to your office, observe their body language. Are they comfortable? Do they look scared? Are they looking at you when they are talking? Are they natural or are they stiff, or pretending to be nice or uncomfortably silent? Observe what you are talking about. Is it about family or about work? Is the conversation loose and flowing? Or is it stiff and jaded? If this employee is uncomfortable, then you are at the very least a jerk to this person. Since this was a random sampling the odds are you are seen as a jerk to more than just one person. If you passed this test or failed this test, do it again, one by one, until you have invited at least 200 people or all of your employees into your office. Too many? Don't have enough time to do this? Guess what? You have a DAM problem. Do you know where the solution to your delivery, service, quality, sales, throughput, profitability, market share, new product development and commercialization, innovation, technology, business systems, and revenue growth problems are? They are within the four walls of your company. If your people aren't talking to you openly and honestly you have no chance to know what the real problems are and you have no chance to find the solutions that will transform your company to greatness.

Great companies are crafted with care under the umbrella of great leadership. Great leaders attract great talent. What is the price to attract people to you? Get rid of your ego DAM! A great leader allows people to see them for who they are. They are brave enough to expose their weaknesses and they are confident enough to talk about their failures. This is what is called humility. Humility is strongly attractive when combined with skill, mastery, and purpose. Humility is a necessary component to any great leader. The remaining chapters of the book discuss how you can be a better person and how you can be a great leader.

Let me give you an example. When I was stuck getting nowhere at Rockwell Collins (Chapter 2) I had to find a solution on how to get unstuck. I had a DAM problem: I was an entitled, righteous, perfectionist, jerk. I was trying to tell Forrest Voss, a senior engineer, with decades more experience than I had, what I wanted done. Everything I was doing was repulsive to Forrest.

I didn't understand the extent I needed him to save my ass and if things kept on going the way they were I would be out of a job. My first step was to stop being a jerk: I am not as good as I pretend. My second step was to stop trying to be perfect: My way isn't the perfect way; in fact there are an infinite number of other right ways to proceed. My third step was to stop being righteous: This isn't just my problem for me to develop my precious solution, but our problem to be worked on together.

My thinking had to change. I had to let go of my Ego DAM where I dreamed I would be lauded over like the great Roman emperor, Trajan. The citizens of Cedar Rapids, Iowa would find a field and erect a 100 foot-high marble column with a life-like statue of me on top with carvings of my many great victories spiraling upward on the column. It's amazing what you can think while up driving between LaCrosse, Wisconsin and Cedar Rapids, Iowa. This fantasy was getting me nowhere. I had to change my DAM thinking. The solution was within my four walls. I had to admit to myself that in the scheme of things I was an insignificant speck of dust in the cosmic universe. Instead of being blown away, I needed to attract another dust speck to me and that was Forrest. And the fastest and easiest way for that to happen was to ask sincerely for his help.

I could not ask for help while perched on top of the great column I imagined in my head. I had to ask for help as if on that farm field in Rochester, Minnesota with the farmer putting the mirror up for me to look into. I had to ask for help in the way I had learned at Dale Carnegie. Only then was I able to sit down and look Forrest square in the eye and say with total sincerity, "I don't know much of anything that can help you right now. I don't know your process, I don't know how you use our material, I don't know what you have to deal with on a day to day basis. In fact I don't even know much about you. Forrest, I need your help. Will you help me understand what you have to deal with and how you use this material? I want to learn, because I am willing to do whatever it takes to help you."

This action, punching a hole in my ego DAM and asking for help, caused all sorts of positive things to happen seemingly all at once. This is why I call such a simple thing, asking for help, a complex solution. Complex solutions cause a chain reaction of positive outcomes. I learned a lot about how our material was used. I learned about other areas of the huge facility and was introduced to a wide spectrum of different people who could help me anytime I asked. I learned a lot about Forrest and what he liked, what his concerns were, and what he believed. We became friends. We watched each others' back. And in so doing the relationship between the two companies became closer. The sales people respected greatly what I was doing and understood the importance of the relationships I was developing there. I rose from insignificant to the account to being protected by the sales force. My position became integral to the account. Trust increased. Service increased. And problems were identified and solved quickly. As a bonus I got to ride a combine and have a Casey's pizza and feed some hogs with John Decker, another engineer in the group. A humble leader can create a growing cascade of positive attributes that lead to exponential growth. And a great leader can emerge at any level of a company. Even at the level of an inexperienced junior technical service representative who didn't know what he is doing, but smart enough to ask for help and shut up and listen.

WHAT'S COMING!

Since the next chapters are important to you, because they are about solutions to DAM problems, let me highlight some important points in each chapter. In chapter 8 we talk about firing your

Rock Star and keeping your Maverick. Doing both of these things will be scary and feel completely unnatural. You will feel heavy-duty resistance and likely experience significant political pressure to do the wrong thing: keep your Rock Star and fire your Maverick. If you do the right thing, as difficult and scary as this will be for you, your company will blossom and grow almost immediately. You will find this astonishing. Nothing is more important than keeping your good people and getting rid of your bad people. A shrewd understanding of who is good and bad for your organization is absolutely essential in order to build a great company. If you don't get this right your company has no chance. Your solution is within your four walls.

Chapter 9 is about being grateful especially during times when we should feel enraged and bitter. We are raised in school with a strong sense of justice and fairness. But life isn't like that. Sometimes it is just unfair. True, we have every right to feel entitled to our My Precious outcome. If the outcome can't be changed then feeling bitter and angry will just be self-destructive. We have to let go. If we don't, our life remains in bondage—stuck in a prison of our own making. Great leaders know how to deal with life's injustice. Take Mahatma Gandhi: *God's protection is rejection.* The very best plan never survives the first bullet anyway. The new road, with the new plan, may prove to be better. What is bad today, may prove to be a gift later. *As our case is new, so we must think anew and act anew.* Your solution is within your four walls.

Chapter 10 is about being an iconoclast. Ever use the word? The word isn't used much in business. And few companies tell head-hunters, "find me an iconoclast now," but they should! The problems preventing your company from growing like a weed are likely because of habits reinforced by false beliefs. It takes a heretic or an iconoclast that has little respect for your belief system to find out what has your company stuck. Even if the belief system you have for your business is true today, it may not be true tomorrow. The world is in constant FLOW. FLOW is a process and *all processes break stuff up*. The fundamental beliefs of your business have to be challenged on an ongoing basis, or you may wind up with a business that booms and then busts. Your solution is within your four walls.

Chapter 11 is about stating and admitting you are incompetent. Scary. Think you might get fired if you tell your boss this? You might. But be honest with yourself: Our jobs are so complex today, it is foolish to think we can do our job without help from others. If you see asking for help as admitting incompetence then you have a DAM problem. If you see it as true that you are incompetent and need everyone's help, then you are a FLOW thinker and have the potential to be a great leader. Admitting honestly what you don't do well and asking someone for help is a very powerful force that will attract good people to you. But be aware: If your boss is a Rock Star who is an entitled, righteous, perfectionist, jerk, you will be fired. And that may prove to be the best thing that ever happened to you. Your solution is within your four walls.

Chapter 12, is about not shooting the messenger. Think problems are negative? Think people bringing problems to you are negative people? Without problems and defining problems we can't find real solutions. When we fail to admit there is a problem and shoot the messenger we not only fail in our business, but we leave ourselves wide open to crisis that in the worst case scenario kills innocent people. The root of all tragedy is when we fail to see the solution that is always within our four walls.

People in business that have run companies for decades who listen to my DAM thinking explanations, like the ego DAM where we want to be seen as better than others, listen to my explanations about the Rock Star who is an entitled, righteous, perfectionist jerk, and how the solution is so close that it is within their four walls, have difficulty understanding why they haven't heard this before. They have difficulty understanding that something so obvious just isn't second nature to us. As a result, they feel entitled to know why this is so. Why they have been deceived or not told the truth? This, by the way, is entitled behavior. It's an attempt to keep the same couch potato thinking. However, it is a natural thought process that starts to break up old ideas. So let me go deeper with you to help speed up your thinking process.

The place to start is with Jazz music. Shortly after World War II, a new type of Jazz music was being played, called be-bop. This music broke all the rules of conventional music with its harmonics, chord substitutions, unusual rhythms, and it's destruction of melodies. *Every process breaks things up* and be-bop was breaking things up. This revolution was lead foremost by Charlie Parker, who was a virtuoso of his instrument, a genius composer and arranger, and a heroin addict. Parker, because of his talent, was the natural leader, but it was movement that was doomed. Why? Because of the bad behavior of Parker. The best talents of the day wanted to play like Parker. They thought the reason why Charlie Parker could play the impossible and compose the impossible was because of his heroin habit. As a result, everyone else decided to try heroin, too. This was a tragedy. They were all looking for a solution that was outside of their four walls. Their lives, including Parker's, unfolded like a Greek tragedy.

The analogy of Charlie Parker to business is John D. Rockefeller and his snake oil salesman father, William Rockefeller. William Rockefeller was not a good man. He abandoned his first wife and left her with six children to raise on her own. He started a bigamous marriage with a second woman in Canada. And then at the same time married a third wife and had two more kids. He made his living preying on the trust of others by saying he had the answer to their pain in the bottled elixir solutions he sold called "Rock Oil," which was a mixture of laxatives and petroleum. He cheated on John D., too, thinking he was providing his son important life lessons: how to take advantage of people's trust and do everything you can to maximize your financial gain despite how it might hurt others.

John D. Rockefeller learned from his father on how to manipulate, lie, and cheat to get away with almost anything. It was John D. Rockefeller's success at ruthlessly accumulating wealth and power that made us a society that had to use a lot of gasoline and everything else that went with it like tar and oil and rubber and plastic. It was his success that created our addiction to oil. Any alternative to needing a car with a gas engine was destroyed by Rockefeller. As Jim Colbert states in *Meet William Rockefeller, Snake Oil Salesman* ...

That is the sinister turn of the modern snake oil salesmen. They not only try to sell us their phony cures for our cancers, they give us the cancer of complete dependence on their system, their resources, their corporations. This is the trick by which John D. and the Rockefeller dynasty and all of their ilk have transformed themselves from two-bit peddlers of phony cure-alls to multi-trillion controllers of our economic reality.

He goes on...

But there is something that the modern day snake oil peddlers—the banksters and the oilmen and the multinationals and the globalists and their lackeys in political power—live in constant fear of...The fear that the public will realize that their tonic is useless and their whole show is just a stage act, and the people run them out of town.

The solution is within your four walls. Consider the mess that General Motors used to be. GM suffered from DAM thinking for decades. They tried firing everyone. They tried robots. They tried moving their factories around. They tried copying more successful automakers. Nothing produced a sustainable result. Why? Because they weren't looking for solutions within their four walls. They were looking for snake oil and it didn't work.

Cars like the Chevy Volt are transformative to GM and they are transformative to us and the world! Their products carry a meaning, and like Apple, they are putting a ding in the universe. For example, what would happen if you were to purchase the new Chevy Volt, which is a 100% electric car, where a gasoline generator is used to extend the range of the car? What would happen if instead of getting 15 miles per gallon we were getting 100, 500, or 1000 miles per gallon of gasoline? What would happen to the fear of running out of oil, the rising price of gasoline, global warming, oil money going to terrorists countries? Is this a technology that John D. would support? Absolutely not. Why? Because the prototype CEO looks only at his own self interest exclusively. This prototypical CEO is at the heart of every business catastrophe and every economic and financial melt down. It's the legacy of the snake oil salesman and it still very much haunts us to this day. It is DAM thinking taken to its full Rock Star extreme.

Consider the demise of Merrill Lynch under the leadership of Stan O'Neal—a numbers guy. When Merrill wanted to figure out how to grow even bigger and take a bite out of Goldman Sachs market share they turned to Stan. After working for GM and then getting an MBA from Harvard, Stan worked at Merrill's junk bond division. Later, he ran the leverage finance division. Then he was promoted to chief financial officer of Merrill. He was lauded as heroic for firing 24,000 employees (feeding the Christians to the Lions) and making Merrill suddenly very profitable. There was nothing creative or strategic in what he did. There was no dash of brilliance. An idiot could have done the same thing. What Stan did goes by a name and it is called business process reengineering. It's sold by consultants that ride in with their dog and pony shows and is bought by the CEO for millions upon millions of dollars. It looks sophisticated and cool, but it is nothing more than firing enough people so you have a lot of profit for a short time. The solution doesn't last. It is snake oil.

The problem when you fire people is what are you going to do to grow the company? In Stan's case his solution was to sell snake oil too, in the financial products devised by people they hired straight out of MIT. He created a tonic where he mixed some bad stuff with some good stuff—junk bonds mixed in with triple grade A investments—should get a return of a junk bond, but with the safety of triple grade A asset. What he created was toxic. If you mix a little cyanide with some water what do you get?

In order to sell this toxic tonic, he had to basically encourage his people to lie—that the investments were solid (when they were not)—that they were perfect (perfectly flawed)—and that they were golden(and would ruin you if you took too much). What did he have to do next? He had to encourage an environment where credit risk was signed off when it should not have been. True, the regulation rules that defined Merrill's conservative and safe positioning remained in place. To get around this he had to create a culture of fear, so some people would lie, deceive, and sign off on the bad paper in order to save their jobs. Not everyone was willing to do this and they left the company or were fired. This of course increased the population of unethical behavior.

What was the net result under Stan O'neal's snake oil leadership born out of the snake oil legacy of the Rockefellers? More than an $8 billion loss. What was Stan's reward for doing such a horrible job? More than $160 million!

Most numbers guys like accountants are known for working in a solitary environment and aren't known for thinking outside of the box, working socially with people, and developing creative ideas with others. Stan was described in this way in many published magazine articles. He was cold and calculating and aloof. He was, point blank, antisocial. He would have failed the test of bringing people into his office. Pleasant, sure. But interested in what you thought as a meager employee working underneath him, goodness no. People like this don't know how the real world works. They think robotically instead of intuitively and artistically.

What happens when you have an artist run a company? You have an Apple or Pixar, both run by the same person, Steve Jobs. A great video in which Steve talks briefly about how Apple operates is on YouTube: http://www.youtube.com/watch?v=f60dheI4ARg& feature=related. If you don't walk away thinking *work is social* after listening to Steve, you may be beyond help.

Let me give you a personal example. I had a client where the CEO was a numbers guy. According to the numbers they had a medical device design and manufacturing division where it was impossible to make enough money to be profitable. Similar to Stan O'neal's strategy, cost cutting was the only way. So people were fired, which decreased the ability to finish projects, which decreased the ability to get new design contracts. Because of the ever escalating losses accelerated by his cost cutting actions, the CEO declared everyone was incompetent and if he could, he would close this division. But because of certain financial obligations, they could not close the doors without risking losing the entire company. For this CEO, everything was numbers, costs, utilizations, and hourly rates. Nothing was about creativity, ideas, thinking outside of the box, improvising, and invention. Nothing was Apple-like. Nothing was about work being social.

I was asked to walk into this desperate situation. The first thing I did was look for a solution. Where did I look? Where I always look, inside the four walls of the business. I looked to the people working there for the answers, because I knew they had to be there, because they always are there. First, I had to immerse myself in their world, see things the way they saw them, and challenge them to start thinking and start looking within their four walls. I attended their meetings, I listened to their complaints, I started working with their negative language and let them know what my standard was for language. If it was just a complaint, it wouldn't get us anywhere, so let's move on. If it was about ideas, let's work with these ideas and see if we might find something. With me spending time with them, breaking bread with them, listening to them, and showing that I did care, they showed me their troubles, they accepted my rules, and we became productive, because I was integrated within their four walls.

I struggled with the idea that there must be a faster way to design and develop medical devices and started up discussions around this every chance I got. Finally, a very smart an extremely creative engineer who was soft spoken told me matter of factly in his office, his domain where I had earned the right to be a welcome guest, that there was a faster way. The faster way was called SCRUM, but it was that it had already been attempted, and failed. We talked more about it, and why it failed. It failed because the solution required different thinking. Instead of everything being controlled by the project manager, it would be controlled by the people actually doing the work. Instead of just the project manager seeing the entire project, the entire team would see the project. Instead of the customer being involved only at the beginning, when requirements are defined and at the end when the device would be qualified, they would be intimately involved during the entire design and development cycle of the product and meet with the team every day. The customer would become a member of a tight-nit collaborative team.

What was the result of this inside-the-walls solution? The people working at this company could take a concept and have a workable product in six to eight months instead of two to three years. This proved to be a huge competitive advantage. So much so that this division went from one that had no hope, to the division with the highest profit and growth potential within the entire company. The solution exists within your four walls—always. Thinking anything else is DAM thinking.

CHAPTER 8

Fire Your Rock Star! Keep Your Mavericks!

I need a... credit card that's got no limit, and a big black jet with a bedroom in it...I am gonna trade this life, for fortune and fame...'Cause we all just wanna be big rock stars, and live in hilltop houses, drivin' fifteen cars...Hey, Hey, I wanna be a rock star.

—**Nickelback**

You need to fire your Rock Star immediately. Don't wait. Almost every company has a Rock Star—a person who is seen as indispensable, who works hard to convince you that he is the only one who has the answers; he is the only one who knows what is right, and the only one who is entitled to take credit for everything good about the business. We talked a lot about the Rock Star mentality in Chapter 5. When you fire your Rock Star you will see a huge improvement in productivity, communication, discovery, freedom, and purpose. The sole purpose of the Rock Star is to construct a reality where he or she is the only person that matters. In actuality, he or she may be extremely unskilled and may not be all that valuable to the company. But if you are not careful, Rock Stars, whether they are highly skilled or not, will make you believe you need them.

A Maverick is a very different thing, and sadly, many companies mistake the Maverick for the Rock Star. What is really sad is many companies fire their Mavericks and keep their Rock Stars! One distinguishing characteristic of Mavericks is that they don't play political games, whereas the Rock Star is often a master at political gamesmanship. To be a Maverick you need to be a highly skilled master in your field. With this mastery comes an impatient, demanding person who doesn't understand why others can't operate at the same intellectual level. Earl Bakken in his small pamphlet for Medtronic employees, *Reflections on Leadership*, put it this way: *One of the knottiest problems the manager of any organization may face is the noisy, disruptive presence of a brilliant Maverick.*

Companies want to fire Mavericks because of their independent and anti-social behavior. Mavericks break the rules. They demean people. They defy their bosses. They are disobedient because they stand for a very high level of excellence and mastery. They demand autonomy, and even though they may not agree or understand their real needs, they absolutely need to work with others to achieve their potential. Richard P. Feynman, the Nobel Prize winning physicist, is a classic Maverick. During the Manhattan Project, he stole combinations to safes used to house top-secret documents. He posed as a gifted safe cracker, but what he actually did was find out where people wrote down the combinations in case they forgot them. Time and time again he uncovered the holes that existed in the security at Los Alamos. This was his pet project that he worked on when he got bored. Feynman could not be managed and he often broke rules. He was a Maverick. Robert Oppenheimer, who brought Mavericks like Feynman into the Manhattan Project, was highly regarded for his management talent and his ability to brilliantly lead such a diverse group, and have them behave as a cohesive team.

Earl advises caution when deciding to fire Mavericks because, if you can manage them well, your company will enjoy a huge benefit. If you can manage them well, your company will soar beyond the reach of your competitors.

So what to do? First, sort out your Rock Stars from your Mavericks. Then, create an environment where the Maverick can flourish within a group of seemingly less capable people. Ask these two questions: 1) Does this difficult person want his or her way in order to control everyone? 2) Does this difficult person want his or her way because he or she knows the right answer? Number one is the Rock Star and number two is the Maverick. As easy as it may seem on paper, it can be very tricky to correctly answer these two questions in the real world.

One area where this is particularly difficult is the realm of software engineers and web designers. Too many of them want to be Rock Stars. Part of the reason for this is the huge successes of Bill Gates, founder of Microsoft; Larry Page, Sergey Brin and Eric Schmidt, founders of Google; and Mark Zuckerberg, founder of Facebook. Their success can easily delude sharp and talented software engineers into thinking that they are entitled to riches and fame.

Let's look at two cases of software engineers and see if you can sort out which is the Rock Star and which is the Maverick. Remember, it is always possible to figure out a way to work with Mavericks and re-engage their talents.

For Case One, we have a middle-aged programmer, highly talented, with experience working for many very high-profile companies. I remember meeting this programmer for the first time. With his earphones on, the music playing on his iPod made him deaf to me. I used my listening and observing skills to build his trust. I stood there for a very long time, just staring and watching. You know you are dealing with either Mavericks or Rock Stars when they continue working and neither acknowledge you nor ask you to leave. This person chose to ignore me. Finally I asked him a question, "What do you think about how the previous programmer approached the design issues and function?" That caused him to turn his head and remove both head phones from his ears.

"Not much," he said. "These people didn't understand how to isolate the circuits. They made the control algorithm much more complicated than it needed to be, and the circuitry used was completely over-engineered. I would have done X, Y, Z. But there is nothing much that can be done now."

After giving me this explanation, sudden irritation ran across his face, likely because he didn't understand why he had to explain anything to me. Why should his work be interrupted just so he could pay attention to me? Why was he wasting his valuable time talking to me? "Who are you? What do you do here?" he asked.

"I am a consultant," I explained. "I work closely with this company on problem projects. I work very closely with the plant manager as well as the CEO and they expect me to keep them apprised of all the details. Transparency and trust are very important to this company. I understand you are on the project team. I'm here to learn about what you are doing and to take this opportunity to introduce myself."

I knew I had failed to build trust by listening and observing because I allowed the programmer to put me on the defensive; I had done too much talking and not enough listening. We were now doing battle like two tennis players across from each other, separated by a net. I had failed to get on the same side of the court as him. He looked irritated and was likely considering how he was going to return my shot. Picking up his iPod he said, "Well clearly nobody here knows what to do. The design and software decisions were made by complete morons. Any competent manager would see this. I take it you are part of management." Game. Set. Match. I lost. With that, he put his headphones back in his ears and went back to his work.

The project I was to steer out of trouble had chewed up its entire multi-million dollar budget, and was only 60% complete. We had met several times with the customer to reorganize the work and reestablish our priorities.

During the first meeting with the team, the software engineer with the headphones spoke up. "You are delusional. This will never work," he said. "You will have to completely redesign the board."

"Why?" I asked.

"I just know and I am the expert," he replied.

"Sorry," I said with great passion and emotion. "I respect your skills and your work. But I need reasons! We can't afford to go back to the drawing board and re-layout the electronics!"

"I just know that the circuitry has never been designed for EMI shielding!" he said equally passionately.

"In what way?"

"You would never understand."

"Look," I said, "I love your expertise. I love your talent. But what you are saying is unacceptable. I need to know why the board is no good now. If not, we aren't changing it. And if there is a shielding problem then explain to me why we can't put all of the electronics in a can? We really can't afford to go back to square one unless you can explain, in detail, your concerns and possible contingencies other than redesigning the board. Even if you make a solid argument that the board has to be redesigned, we aren't going to blindly take your word for it. We will verify with data first. And only after that, will we redesign the board."

Again he said, "You just don't understand." And then went silent.

I was beginning to think I was talking with someone from Enron. The software engineer was really telling me to put my *blind trust* in him, that I needed to accept whatever he said. That wasn't going to happen. *Trust, but verify*, was fundamental to the transparency required for the SCRUM process we were using to get this project back on track.

I found out after this meeting that the engineer was very upset with me. He thought I had spoken very rudely to him and he was very irritated that I would challenge his position. What he failed to realize was everyone on that team had the shared purpose of completing the project. He was more worried about how his technical reputation had been challenged than the success of the project—his Feelings DAM was getting in the way of the purpose of the team.

Following the meeting, he pulled me aside, "You have to change the way you are managing this group," he said. "I did not like how you talked to me in this meeting. I demand an apology. And you have to back down on what you are asking the team to do. You don't know squat about how to design a product and you have no right to lead these meetings."

His comments were unpleasant, but not unexpected. Clearly he didn't see the value of a manager for any project!

"I apologize if I offended you," I said, "but I will not change how I am conducting these meetings because they are working. You have your job to do. I have my job to do. We all have to work together to do what we said we would do, to rapidly complete this project. If you don't like that you have the option to leave."

And, within ten minutes that is exactly what he did. He walked off the job with no explanation until people started to call him at home. He demanded my resignation. He was absolutely right that the board needed to be redesigned. He was either following an expert hunch and didn't know why it needed to be redesigned or he just chose not to share his reasoning with his team.

When asked who he might recommend to complete the work he said, "Nobody. I am the best at what I do. Anyone else will just make a mess of it. I am the only one in the world qualified to do the job right."

Was this person a Maverick or a Rock Star? It's a tough call isn't it?

Consider Case Two. Another software engineer was called in to continue the work that the original engineer had abandoned. Similar to case one, this software engineer worked in isolation. If he spoke with you, it was on his terms. He, and only he, was the expert. One day, he came up to me in the hallway. He said, "The work done by the other engineer was unacceptable," he said. "Only I know the right way to make this work." "Well we are blessed to have you be working with us," I said. Underneath my breath I muttered, "All Hail Caesar!"

The first problem with this engineer happened when a mistake with accounts payable kept him from being paid. The engineer was furious. The plant manager worked feverishly to have a check cut but it had to be delivered from the corporate accounts payable office several thousands of miles away. This meant the check would take one day to arrive. The plant manager called the engineer to his office thinking he could apologize and explain how the check would arrive the next morning. The engineer was furious and demanded payment before lunch. If he didn't receive his check, he was going to leave.

So the plant manager said, "I will cut you a cashier's check out of my own bank account and have it to you after I have lunch."

After lunch, the plant manager returned with the check in hand to find the engineer gone. The plant manager couldn't reach him by phone so he sent out an e-mail explaining that his check was at the office. The plant manager also wrote that with the delivery of the check, he expected an update on all current activities and what activities remained in order to have the work completed. The tone of the e-mail and the manager's demands did not sit well with this extremely entitled engineer, who called in the next day and told the manager that the company was in breach of his contract and he wanted a new one that paid double his current rate. On top of this, all payments would be required one week in advance. It would be his option to accept the check and do the work if he decided it was required or reject the check and work for another client at another company. If he didn't receive the pre-payment, he wouldn't do any work.

This engineer wanted the power to decide how much he would be paid, when he would be paid, and whether he was going to work or go on holiday. He didn't want any contract that obligated him to his client, and wanted the power to declare whether or not his client was in breach of contract and had failed in its obligations to him. As in Rome, all Caesars must be paid their tithing. All Caesars must maintain ultimate power. All Hail Caesar!

As you might have guessed, Case One was the Maverick and Case Two was the Rock Star. The Maverick was all about the work and being acknowledged for his good work (Mavericks love praise). Mavericks want respect for their expertise and have no tolerance for being challenged by those who aren't equally knowledgeable. Mavericks make rash decisions. They are completely blocked by the Feelings DAM when things don't go their way in a technical area. It is then that all heck breaks loose with the Maverick. People who are really skilled can get Mavericks to consider them as friends, not adversaries or competition. Mavericks must have turf they call their own or they just won't be happy. But at the same time they need to collaborate with people in order to reach their full potential. So it isn't easy figuring out how to manage and keep your Maverick.

With the Rock Star all heck breaks loose right from the get-go. Anything can set off a Rock Star. When you work with a Rock Star, you learn to walk on egg shells. Rock Stars aren't satisfied until they have complete and total control of everything. Rock Stars don't often care about acknowledgement for doing a good technical job, they just want money and power, and can't ever have too much. Rock Stars couldn't care less about your company or the people in it. They may or may not be technically skilled, but they will be much more protective about what they are doing than the Maverick. Unlike the Maverick, who usually has a few confidantes, Rock Stars typically don't have anyone. They love to talk to anyone who will listen, as often as they can, about how superior and indispensable they are.

The problem with Rock Stars is that, at first, they seem to have good qualities, such as a strong work ethic. For example, they show up on time each and every day, put in their time, and do very consistent and predictable work. And they seem to be self-reliant and able to make decisions without your involvement. But, then you start to notice that you no longer know what they are doing. You don't know what they are saying to your customers or suppliers. And your other employees start to worry because somehow the Rock Star has convinced them he is in charge, not you.

You see a hint of a problem but you aren't sure what it is. Suddenly you lose control and don't know why. This can happen extremely quickly. The plant manager with the Rock Star engineer lost almost an entire week when his number one priority, which then turned into his only priority, was to make the Rock Star happy. And what he found was just how impossible it is to make a Rock Star happy. Unknowingly, the plant manager fell into the gigantic Feelings DAM of the Rock Star.

Often companies don't realize they have a Rock Star. I remember conducting an assessment interview with a CEO who had a problem employee. In the middle of our interview he said "I'm not sure Gray, but I think I have a problem with a particular person."

"Explain to me what you mean by 'problem,'" I replied.

He said, "I want to take the company in a new direction, but this person fights against it every time I bring it up. I need him to complete his current project but he won't do it. He says he needs to be with me, to help me and guide me in important decisions. I am beginning to feel there's something odd about this. It is as if I am working for him."

"Does he insist on being a part of every meeting you have where important decisions are to be made?"

"Yes."

"Does every decision you make have to meet with his approval?"

After a long pause he said, "Come to think of it, yes."

"Does he reject requests you make of him, be it what he is to work on, or even how to talk or present to a customer or client?"

"Yes."

"Well," I said. "I think you have a Rock Star. Rock Stars are often jerks to others. They require perfection before any attempt to move forward is made. They judge others harshly and have no tolerance for being judged. They feel entitled to higher pay, special perks, and other special treatments. They want absolute control of anything important going on with your company."

"Wow," he replied. "I have a Rock Star. But I can't fire him because he is so important."

"There are some things you can do to test if this person can change for the better," I said, "but I must warn you, the probability of success is low and you will lose valuable time. Firing your Rock Star is very scary, but in every case I have witnessed, the boss is amazed as other employees step in and fill the void."

You have to fire your Rock Star. Rock Stars have their fingerprints on as much in your company as possible so firing them may seem impossible. They will do everything they can to seem infinitely valuable. In doing this they make everyone else's life miserable. Even so, they make others in the company believe they are indispensable, so firing a deeply entrenched Rock Star is probably the scariest thing you can do. Yet every instance I have been involved in, firing the Rock Star resulted in huge improvements. Employees were happier. Customers were happier. And surprisingly enough, the business not only didn't collapse, it throve.

Unfortunately, in too many companies the Rock Star is the CEO. Companies that have a Rock Star as the CEO have a serious DAM problem.

Before we leave this chapter, I know what you might be thinking. You don't want to fire your Rock Star, because you think you can save him. You want to fire your Maverick, because you think you can survive without her, and everything would be so much more comfortable. Often the move that feels right and comfortable in any discipline, be it golf, playing the piano, or business, is the wrong one.

Let me tell you a story that Frank Delk likes to share with me. If you watch a flock of geese on the ground eating, you will notice almost all of them have their heads facing a small patch on the ground. You will see at least one goose that has his head up looking far out at a great distance from the flock. The view this goose sees is very much different than the geese feeding on the ground. Without that one goose, the flock is in great danger. And they won't know it until it is way too late. That one goose is your Maverick. They are the one person who can see out five or ten years or more and put your company ahead by light years. And if you fire your Maverick while your competition listens to their Maverick and manages her productively, then you aren't going to know what hit you until it is way too late. All great innovative companies have at least one maverick.

If you try to save the Rock Star, because you or somebody above you thinks they are absolutely indispensable, you are in trouble. The logical question is whether it is possible to rehabilitate the Rock Star. And yes there might be less than a handful of people capable of doing it. You will have to spend a million if not millions of dollars, dollars you don't have because the Rock Star is costing you a million or millions of dollars. So no, don't go there. It just isn't good business.

CHAPTER 8 SUMMARY

In any company, Rock Stars are difficult from the moment they are hired. Rock Stars want to get involved in too many things; they don't respect other people or their work. From day one they boast about how important they are. Rock Stars care about themselves; they couldn't care less about you or your company.

The reason companies hire Rock Stars is because they don't look at the character of the person. Instead they believe his boasts and claims that, initially, are very seductive. A Rock Star is typically very good at selling herself. Despite how much you may think you need the Rock Star, you don't. Don't hire her. If you have hired her, you need to fire her. It may be the scariest thing you ever do in business, but you will find everyone else will step up to the plate and fill in the void.

Mavericks are easy to mistake for Rock Stars. Mavericks are very difficult to manage. They may or may not have all of the Thinking DAMs, but they are usually very impatient with people. They expect their expertise to be respected. And they expect special treatment. They understand their field of study and are true experts. They can contribute greatly to any company. They typically aren't very good at selling themselves. They typically aren't very good with people. And they typically have good friends who understand their idiosyncrasies, watch out for them and protect them from others and themselves. How you manage them is a book all in itself. But at the end of the day, you want to fire your Rock Star and keep your Maverick.

WHAT WOULD BE GOOD ABOUT FIRING YOUR ROCK STAR?

Instructions: Find a partner so you get used to life without the Ego DAM. If shame works for you, then I am incredibly disappointed in you if you don't have a partner. We are now walking down the pyramid and becoming better people. A strong step in making a positive change is to spend a few days or longer just thinking about all the positive benefits of not having your Rock Star around. Do not think about any of the negative outcomes until you have spent significant time thinking about the positive outcomes. This will help you overcome the fear of firing your Rock Star.

With the removal of the Rock Star you would find...

1= Meaningless 2= OK 3= Some Benefit 4= Big Benefit 5= Life Changing

➤ The ability to focus on the business would be?

| | 1 | 2 | 3 | 4 | 5 |

➤ The ability to focus on other employees and their needs would be?

| | 1 | 2 | 3 | 4 | 5 |

➤ Having more control of the business decisions would be?

| | 1 | 2 | 3 | 4 | 5 |

➤ Less evidence of demoralized employees would be?

| | 1 | 2 | 3 | 4 | 5 |

➤ Opening territory for others to step in and see what they could do would be?

| | 1 | 2 | 3 | 4 | 5 |

➤ Setting standards and holding everyone accountable without the subversive tactics of the Rock Star would be?

| | 1 | 2 | 3 | 4 | 5 |

➤ The ability to be sensitive to customer's needs instead of the Rock Star's needs would be?

| | 1 | 2 | 3 | 4 | 5 |

➤ Having more transparency in the organization without the hidden agendas of the Rock Star would be?

| | 1 | 2 | 3 | 4 | 5 |

➤ Employees being able to ask for help without experiencing the ridicule, permission, or inquisition of the Rock Star would be?

| | 1 | 2 | 3 | 4 | 5 |

➢ Being able to create SCRUM teams and Masterminds so that people can be more intelligent and more effective would be?

1   2   3   4   5

19 or below

You either don't have a Rock Star or you're not concerned about the impact the Rock Star is having on your business. A low score here is not a good thing. Careful listening and observing should provide you with clues as to the dynamics created because of the Rock Star.

20 to 39

You see benefit from making a change. Listen and observe what is going on for a week or two in your company. List other positive benefits for not having your Rock Star. Be careful that you haven't identified a Maverick. One differentiator is that a Maverick very rarely wants to get into your business. A Rock Star does. After you have considered all the positive benefits of not having a Rock Star for at least several days attempt to make a list of what would be good about keeping your Rock Star. This should provide you with more motivation to do what has to be done.

40 or Above

You definitely see the value of making a change. Your next step is to write down what you fear will happen if you fire your Rock Star. Interview for a replacement, and look for FLOW thinking traits. The last thing you want to do is hire another Rock Star. Consider what benefits this new person will bring to the table. If you don't plan on replacing this individual, then come up with a plan how other people can step up to the plate. In my experience, you will likely be very surprised at how people will step up when the Rock Star leaves and your company will become much better, very quickly.

CHAPTER 9

God's Protection is Rejection

---

*A proud man is seldom a grateful man, for he never thinks
he gets as much as he deserves.*

—Henry Ward Beecher

A very successful CEO once told me that his company had something really good going for it and also something bad. The good thing was that a lot of employees had worked for his company a very long time. The bad thing was that a lot of employees had worked for his company a very long time.

Many well-established companies that experience slower growth than in the past have loyal employees with an attitude of entitlement. This naturally happens if Thinking DAMs aren't actively managed. Entitled employees believe you and your company owe them. If you break this rule, then the trust they had in you and the company is violated. A mentality of entitlement is a difficult thing to unwind. What you need to set in motion from the beginning is a culture of surprise gratefulness. This is why you should reconsider annual incentive programs or bonuses.

A dentist once told me how he chose to run his office. "I never give Christmas bonuses," he said, "because, no matter what, my employees would expect it each and every year. If they didn't get one, they would be angry with my practice and with the patients. Instead, what I do is give them a surprise bonus when the business is doing well and they are doing a good job. I say, good job, and nothing more. Afterwards, they don't know when (or if) they will receive a bonus and they are always grateful when they do. In this way, the bonus becomes a motivator. It also makes it fun to work here because people like to be surprised."

What should you do to get rid of this entitlement infestation if you have it? You might reset the standard of your expectations and your employees' expectations by saying,

"Anything can happen on any particular day. Good things can happen. Bad things can happen. Many things happen outside of our control. This company could be bought or sold. We could all lose our jobs, because of that. A meteor could hit the Earth or a great volcano could erupt, ripping up a large fraction of the Earth's crust. Many events could happen tomorrow that wipe us all off the planet. Be grateful for being alive. Be grateful for what you have right now. You can never be absolutely certain. And there is never absolute certainty in business. That is the nature of the game. A game you have chosen to play with this company. Sometimes things will go well. Sometimes things will go bad. But at all times we have to work together. And I, as your leader, am truly grateful you are here with me, to work with me, to grow with me."

Sometimes the best thing that can happen to a company is a crisis. Crises are amazing. Sometimes they destroy people and companies. Other times they become the catalyst for amazing growth.

I have seen great things happen in business. Shipley used to outsource all of the manufacturing of its products to a chemical company. All of a sudden the chemical company decided it would continue to make the product but sell it under its own name and brand, and cut Shipley off completely from its existing customers! I don't know if the intent was to cause Shipley to fail, but the effect was devastating. Shipley had to scramble to improve their existing product so it was better than that of their former supplier, now their competitor. Then they had to figure out how to manufacture the product at the volume their customers expected. If they couldn't do either of these quickly, they would lose all of their business.

To its extreme credit, Shipley chose to become maximally productive. People were focused. They moved fast. They collaborated. They dealt with the immediate reality. They trusted each other, fought like gladiators and were extremely happy and grateful for the positive outcome.

The company started to FLOW and flow fast. What emerged was a much stronger and more highly respected specialty chemical company that had the confidence to make anything happen. During a crisis, many companies find that their people perform brilliantly, decisions are made quickly, and everything flows. And for many decades Shipley flowed and grew in the wake of the worst business crisis it could ever possibly imagine.

From this example comes a great truth from which we all can benefit once we understand it. It is a saying of Mohandas Gandhi that confused me for decades: *God's Protection is Rejection.*

I remember when I was fired (technically called "being reassigned") from the APM division of Monsanto. It was 1996. Marty Rapp, now the CEO of Laird Technologies, called us to line up outside of his office. Our small division needed to cut costs. It needed to look good on paper for a potential buyer. I worked very hard and had done extremely good work. I really didn't consider the possibility I would be fired. I believed I was entitled to my job because I had done it well. Anything else just wouldn't be right; it wouldn't be fair.

So when I walked into Marty's office, and he asked, "What do you think Gray? Are you staying or are you going?"

I said with great confidence, "I am staying."

Marty, confused by my sense of confidence, looked at me and said, "No, you are going."

I couldn't hear anything more. I remember driving home like a zombie, turning my computer on like a zombie, and playing a computer game like a zombie. I felt better after the large severance check but even so, I felt unjustly treated. And though I did not fly into a rage, I felt alone. I didn't want to talk about it. And if I did talk about it, the anger I was trying to hide boiled beneath the surface, making me less than what I was capable of being. At the time I didn't know what to do other than let time heal the wound. Later, I discovered the meaning of *God's Protection is Rejection* and it has helped me ever since.

On September 11th, 2001, my clock radio went off. I heard a low rumbling in the background and the voice of an announcer saying, "And now the second tower of the World Trade Center has collapsed."

What?!

I turned on the TV as the morning sun began to filter through the windows of my bedroom. It was going to be a beautiful day but that didn't matter now. I picked up the phone and started dialing.

My mind couldn't grasp what had happened that day. As I did my errands, everything seemed so quiet. Nobody crowded me on the road. I wanted to go up to strangers and just shake their hands. I wanted to look people in the eye and say, "It's OK."

I wanted to hear the same from them too. I was at my absolute best with other people that day. And apparently I wasn't alone.

In the PBS Broadcast, *Faith and Doubt at Ground Zero,* Helen Tworkov comments,

> *These stories of people waiting for their friends or not leaving their friends, or walking out in such peaceful lines, and these firemen and these policemen running upstairs to help people, and the way people treated each other—where did all of that come from? It was just there.*

Something good emerged from that crisis. We saw people at their absolute best. Some felt their faith reinforced by the outpouring of kindness. Sometimes, in the midst of absolute chaos and tragedy, our best selves emerge.

However, some deeply faithful people also found their beliefs challenged. People of very deep and strong religious faith can lose their faith if they aren't careful, because their strong beliefs become entitlements.

Joseph Griesedieck, an Episcopal Priest, had this to say:

> *Some have said to me, 'I was so materialistic. I'm trying to be more spiritual,' whatever that means. Those are the positive changes ... There are other changes that I'm not pleased to see, and some of those changes are in myself—a deepened sense of cynicism, a sense of being alone more than before ... To be vulnerable is very difficult right now. And to be open to faith takes vulnerability....*

These are totally different reactions to the same horrific event. One person saw the best of people emerge from a tragedy that symbolized the worst way we can treat each other. The other saw how others pulled something good out of the worst tragedy imaginable, but for him, a great trust—a belief in what he thought he was entitled to—was broken. And what was broken threatened to break the man and his faith.

Tragedy is a great test. It challenges how we think. How we respond to tragedy defines us to the very core. Once we see who we really are, we have the opportunity to become stronger. This is what Gandhi understood. *God's protection is rejection.* Any person filled with entitlement will have a very difficult time growing after a tragedy. A grateful person stands a very good chance of emerging stronger after a tragedy and, as a result, being more protected from tragedy in the future.

When I was young, I remember flying into temper tantrums when I was denied something to which I felt entitled. Tears ran down my face as I demanded justice and fairness. My dad, amused, looked me in the eye, and with his feelings in complete control, he would say, "Son, life isn't fair."

My dad was trying to teach me to reframe the obvious negative situation I was experiencing into something positive, to accept the situation and deal with reality creatively rather than destructively, and to use injustice to improve my life. It is a difficult lesson to learn. It takes strength to feel gratitude for what we have received in an environment of rejection. It takes strength to use injustice as a positive force. When we think God has rejected us, it takes strength to dig deep and find the jewel that provides a greater meaning, a meaning that offers great protection.

It's one thing to understand what I am saying about gratefulness in an intellectual way, but to understand it emotionally requires more than mere intellect. In order for you to really get it, I must take you to a very emotional place. Once there, I encourage you to find a personally emotional place of your own to use.

I remember the time I was at the *Windows on the World* Restaurant at the top of the North Tower of the World Trade Center, pressing my face against the window and looking down. When things have really gone bad for me, I mentally placed myself back up on that high building, only this time the date is September, 11th, 2001. I feel the heat of the flames at my back; the thick smoke makes it hard for me to breathe. Once again, I look down from the dizzying height, this time with the window broken. I try to imagine what I would do, what my behavior would be in such an awful circumstance.

I remember images of the jumpers who plunged to their deaths on that terrible day. Nobody likes to talk about the jumpers, the people who chose to jump from the highest floors in order to escape the heat and the smoke. Photographers took pictures of them, pictures that are hard to look at because they could have been any of us!

One image is particularly poignant to me—a man and woman holding hands before they jumped. They continued to hold hands while they were falling. One person could have been an executive. The other could have been a clerk. Their positions, their jobs, everything they thought important, didn't matter anymore. The crisis had wiped out everything they had, in an instant. In an instant, their 'everything' was reduced to nothing! No hope! No future! Nothing! Instead of choosing to be angry, crying, or being full of self pity, they made a powerful decision that serves as an example for all of us. With what little time they had, they chose to live their remaining moments in the most comforting and loving way they could. When I think of them and try to imagine what it must have been like, I am supremely grateful for what I have right now in this moment, no matter what the situation.

God's Protection is Rejection.

Though we can grow from a bad experience, deliberate exposure to bad things can kill us. In the May, 2011 issue of National Geographic, I saw a man free climbing, by himself, upside down (no rope, just hands and feet) on a rock thousands of feet in the air above Yosemite Valley. If he failed, he died. There was no chance to re-learn and do it over. When I looked at the picture I wanted to scream, "Use a rope!" Many climbers, many expert skiers, many daredevils, die young. They die in spectacular and tragic ways. They die because they create a crisis that has no recovery. Crises always have the same fingerprint, be it a climber falling to his death, Chernobyl blowing up, or AIG and the banking crisis. If we succeed doing something once that is full of risk, we believe we can succeed again at the same risky thing. When we feel entitled, we think the probability of survival is 100%, even though, in reality, it may only be 1%. Why do we think we are bulletproof? When we survive the climb we feel overconfident; our success so far is 100%! And then one day, something slips, and we die. A feeling of entitlement can kill.

I once took some friends out four-wheel driving down an Arizona road to the Verde River. With difficulty, we made the first crossing, then headed north on a desolate, muddy road that circumscribed the east side of Horseshoe Reservoir towards a beautiful footbridge called Sheep's Bridge. Everything was going fine. My friends, Anita, Missy, and Cindy were having a blast taking pictures. My long-arm lifted Jeep with a tri-link in the back was not your normal vehicle. You had to take a very large step and pull with all of your might to get into the thing.

I wanted a land vehicle that could go over anything and go through everything. I wanted to make a second crossing of the river at the bridge and return on a different route. I felt entitled to make that crossing because I had never failed to do so in the past.

Arizona rivers are tricky. The water level can change frequently and unless there is a well known landmark in the middle it can be difficult to tell from the bank how much the water level has changed. The current can also gouge and move the river bottom.

I noticed some differences from my earlier crossing but ignored what I was seeing because I knew my vehicle could cross this river. I had done it before, and I was entitled to do it again!

But when I entered the river, I soon realized my mistake. My Jeep was going down like a submarine. I felt like an idiot, but I didn't have time to think; I had to exit. After some effort I got the door open, fell into the river, and went forward to get the winch cable at the front of the vehicle.

With the help of the women, and after many attempts, we were able to begin pulling the Jeep out sideways, but we could not get it completely out of the water. It was a tense situation and we easily could have lost our composure. I could have screamed, "I am such an idiot! Why did I try this?" or "It should have worked!" Anita, Missy, and Cindy could have shouted, "We had plans for dinner; plans for visiting friends later; plans for being well rested for our flights tomorrow, and look what you have done with your foolish attempt! You idiot!"

Everybody had a right to feel entitled to a different future but it wasn't going to happen. Nobody complained. Everyone thought of options, and there weren't many. I was immensely impressed with my friends who showed great strength, leadership, and teamwork to get us out safely.

After many attempts in the river, I was starting to show obvious signs of early onset of hypothermia. Anita put her foot down and said, "Stop, we are walking."

I stared at the Jeep and resigned myself to the fact that it was stuck. I had to deal with the immediate reality and listen seriously to the order given by Anita. Our only option was to walk back down the muddy road towards a ranch that was about 10 miles away, and get ourselves within cell phone range so we could call someone to help us. After I changed into a dry coat and sweat shirt, we started to walk. The sky was turning different shades of reds, oranges, and purples as the sun set behind the mountains. The mud caused us to slip as we tried to reach stable ground. By the time night fell, the Milky Way looked down upon us. It was a fantastic site that cast an eerie shadow on a large, precarious section where the road disappeared into a wash.

Working as a team, we located the road on the other side of the wash. At that point we were on mile six of the walk. By mile nine, it started to get cold. The night was quiet and dark when, with very little battery power left in our phone, we dialed 911.

The operator tried to be helpful but she couldn't understand the circumstance we were in. "What is the closest intersection?" she asked. "What mile marker are you at? What do you see in front of you?"

She finally realized we were lost out in the wilderness of Arizona and told us help was on the way. Knowing we were getting close to the ranch, we continued to walk. Up to this point, it had been almost four hours. It was quiet. There was nothing around us. And everything was still.

Then we heard the sound of a helicopter coming over the mountains in the distance. I called 911 again. "Did you send a helicopter for us?" I asked.

"Yes," the operator replied.

With no flare or match, we couldn't make a signal to catch the pilot's attention. The helicopter came towards us, went away from us, east, then west, north, and south. Finally Anita came up with a great idea and shot off her digital camera flash. Instantly the helicopter spotted us, and carefully landed well in front of us. At this point, Missy said, "I will have such a great story to tell back home! This will beat anybody's story hands down!" When you are from Zumbrota, Minnesota, the middle of farm country, not too far from Rochester, and especially when you are a teenager there is a friendly competition for the best story. Missy knew she had scored a huge prize. I just hoped nobody back in Zumbrota would erect a statue to my idiocy.

The helicopter landed, its great white light shining on us as if we were in the Steven Spielberg movie, *Poltergeist*. Jokingly, I told everyone, "Don't go into the light, stay away from the light." Then we saw the silhouette of our rescuer walking slowly toward us.

Missy said, "Thank you! Thank you! Thank you! What is your name?"

"Hold on," he replied. He spoke into the radio, "All accounted for." He turned back to Missy, "My name is Eric."

"I am going to name my first born after you," said Missy.

I wasn't proud of the entitlement trap I had fallen into, but I was very proud of my friends and the way we conducted ourselves while getting out of a very messy situation. By listening to each other, working together, not having any Thinking DAMs, and not beating each other up for what we felt entitled to, we escaped a dangerous situation without harm.

Is it possible to learn without a traumatic event or placing oneself or others in dangerous situations? If you choose to hang on to your Thinking DAMs then only through recovering from an extreme event will you have any chance to learn, change, and grow. When we get ourselves in trouble, like I did with my Jeep, we make decisions in isolation. We fail to elicit options. As a result, no matter how high our IQ, we do something stupid. We fail. We fail to see the people right in front of us. We fail to ask them for help. We fail to collaborate with them. We fail to mastermind with them. We fail to ask them a most simple and basic question, "What do you think?" and then shut up and listen. Why? We think we are better than them. We think we know it all. We think it's our responsibility and not theirs to make our precious decision. We don't trust their background, gender, or maybe even race, so we don't ask.

What would have happened if I asked the three women some simple open-ended questions? What do you think? What do you see? What should we do? Even though they didn't know Arizona rivers, even though they didn't understand how my Jeep was modified, I would have tapped into a huge resource of knowledge. One was an expert at the outdoors and survival; the second was an expert on farm machinery and equipment. The third was an expert on pushing the limits and having fun. This combination would have made a great mastermind, but I chose to make my decision in isolation. As a result I lost my Jeep and learned my lesson the hard way. And I am the author of this book! I am not immune to DAM thinking. I am just like you! I need help too!

How do we fix this? The article in National Geographic with the climber risking his life was titled, *Daring, Defiant, Free*. We struggle with the force of wanting to be autonomous from everyone and everything and knowing we did it ourselves to show the world we are the best. Who doesn't get passionately inspired by the words, daring, defiant, free? But if we lived these words each and every day we would die young like the Rock Star. We absolutely need people. The absolute true reality is we are social creatures. If we weren't that way our species would have been extinct long ago. So we struggle with the equal and opposite forces. We need to be collaborative with people, to receive support, guidance, wisdom, and inspiration. One force is about our need for autonomy and being antisocial and the other force is about our need for collaboration and being social. We need both or we will die. So there is no fixing it. We just have to get better at learning about our needs and how we manage ourselves.

When we can ask for help, learn something from others, drop the barriers we protect, and trust others, we will experience a wonderful world. We won't even see the rejection anymore. We will just see God's protection all around us. I am very grateful for the loss of my jeep and for the river rejecting my attempt to cross it. Because of my self-inflicted crisis, it made me a much better and safer person who can ask for help even more freely.

CHAPTER 9 SUMMARY

Good things happen. Bad things happen. How we feel about both these things steers our life in a good way or in a bad way. When we practice being grateful for both good things and bad things we can produce, we can discover, we can grow, and we can communicate. When we practice being entitled to both good things and bad things then we can't produce, we can't discover, we can't grow, and we can't communicate. We are stuck. It comes down to a choice. Do we choose to feel bitter about what we should have had? Do we choose to feel bitter about what we lost? Or do we choose to find the strength from the statement that God's protection is rejection?

It's almost impossible for us to recover from a traumatic event and be the same person. In fact, our sense of entitlement is often the driving force that creates messes in our own lives. And if we aren't careful, our own strong sense of entitlement just might kill us, because we are delusional about the risk. What protects us then? What keeps our need for autonomy—being daring, being defiant, and being free—in check? If we change for the better then we have learned something incredibly valuable. Do we need to create our own traumatic event from which to learn? No.

When we isolate ourselves and expect things to happen, the thing will always be less than what it could be. Granted it could be spectacular, but likely we had help from friends or a coach or a mentor. Nothing much can happen in isolation. We reach our full potential as human beings by being social—by being collaborative. We might find the word rejection stripped from our vocabulary. Instead we see unlimited possibilities, because of all the resources at our disposal. This defines yet another meaning behind *God's protection is rejection.*

WHAT WOULD BE GOOD ABOUT BEING MORE GRATEFUL?

Instructions: Ok. Did you find a partner? If you haven't found a partner yet, I don't think you are getting much out of this book. You should set it down and do something else until you find someone who can *help* you. Ok. We need to take another step down so we can have better companies, so we can be better people, and allow our people to grow. As before, think only about all of the positive outcomes for being grateful. Do not think about any of the negative outcomes for being grateful for at least several days. I think you will discover that there are strong reasons to be more grateful in your life.

By replacing your feelings of rejected entitlement and replacing them with gratefulness you would find...

1= Meaningless 2= OK 3= Some Benefit 4= Big Benefit 5= Life Changing

➢ The ability to be more productive and more open to people much sooner after a traumatic event would be?

1   2   3   4   5

➤ The ability to learn from others that have gone through a similar traumatic event would be?

1   2   3   4   5

➤ The ability to be open to all the learning possibilities from the event would be?

1   2   3   4   5

➤ The ability to learn from others and their mistakes rather than repeating them in your own life would be?

1   2   3   4   5

➤ The ability to honestly express your sincere gratitude to your employees, which would build trust and morale would be?

1   2   3   4   5

➤ Having a grateful, more stable work force that is more tolerant of business decisions would be?

1   2   3   4   5

➤ An ability to ask for help from anyone and express your gratitude for their willingness to help would be?

1   2   3   4   5

➤ Being grateful for surviving rather than feeling entitled to do something risky again would be?

1   2   3   4   5

➤ Opportunity to create surprise at work rather than entitlement to a bonus which can only lead to disappointment would be?

1   2   3   4   5

➤ Having a focused work force rather than a bickering work force arguing over what is fair and unfair would be?

1   2   3   4   5

19 or below

You see no advantage to feeling grateful.

20 to 39

You see a benefit to change. Congratulations. Think about it some more and write down (with your partner) other reasons why. Then pick something you have been struggling with, like being fired, or not getting promoted, or something in your personal life. Take just one thing and start thinking about it differently. What change did this bad thing in your life create? What are the things you can feel grateful for? This might sound like making lemonade from lemons, but the simple fact of the matter is that old common sense remedies work.

40 or Above

Wow. You see real benefit to being grateful. Congratulations, because if you had feelings of entitlement before they will likely disappear soon. Read the paragraph above and do everything there. But then try to be more open to people and realize they need help too. Realize by expressing your sincere gratitude to them, you are likely helping them too. We are all social creatures. We all need each other. And when we discover this in our businesses then seemingly anything becomes possible.

CHAPTER 10

Be an Iconoclast!

Most people are other people. Their thoughts are someone else's opinions, their lives a mimicry, their passions a quotation.

—Oscar Wilde

Why do parents want their kids to grow up to be doctors? Why don't parents encourage their kids to be authors instead?

It's all about certainty. The last thing you want to do as a parent is to send your kid out into a territory filled with risk. Our need to protect our family comes from an emotional place—not a rational place. For example, my father turned down his Rhode's Scholarship because his dad said, "Authors are poor and you won't make a good living at it. You must be a doctor, otherwise your future will be bleak."

This is the very definition of the My Precious DAM. We judge what is right and wrong in our territory in order to protect it from danger. Despite these good intentions, we wind up living a life based on a lie instead of the truth. We wind up hurting the very people we are trying to protect, including ourselves.

The need to protect spills into our work life. We have an egioc emotional response instead of a mindful, rational response to new ideas. The new idea is the enemy. The status quo is our friend. People who do just the opposite, embrace new ideas and challenge the status quo—the Iconoclast—are to be shunned.

What is an Iconoclast? It is someone who destroys religious symbols or established dogma or conventions.

Iconoclasts exhibit the exact behaviour you need to make your company great. They are at the source of the discovery that will propel your company light years past your competition. Despite this proven fact, I have yet to see a company post, "Iconoclast wanted here!" In fact, for the Iconoclast, the message often is, "Please go away. You make our lives extremely uncomfortable."

Closed, righteous thinking collides abruptly with the open curious mind of the Iconoclast. They don't mix.

I remember sitting in my dorm room at St. Olaf College. I was trying to read Fyodor Dostoyevsky's *The Brothers Karamazov*, a book about which my philosophy teacher, Howard Hong said, "If the Bible had never been written, this book would take its place." There was a knock on my door. I opened it. A student tour guide came walking in with a prospective student and her parents.

The father, asked, "What is that book you are reading?"

"It's *The Brothers Karamazov*," I said.

"I have never heard of it," he said. "Why are you reading it?"

I didn't bother to answer. He then wanted to know why I liked this St. Olaf's. As soon as I started to answer he looked down at his watch. Trying to ignore his insult, I explained why I chose this school and why I liked it, including how I had found the history department to be provocative and energizing.

He immediately interrupted and said, "What kind of job is anyone going to get studying history?"

At that time Malcolm Gladwell, the best selling author of *Blink, The Tipping Point,* and *Outliers,* was up in Trinity College in Toronto majoring in History. I suspect this man standing in my dorm room, looking at his Rolex, wouldn't have anything nice to say about this scrawny, odd looking, middle distance runner, who someday wanted to write for the New Yorker. He would likely condemn Malcolm Gladwell for wanting to study history in the same way that my grandfather condemned my dad's passionate desire to go to Oxford under a Rhode's scholarship to study English.

The truth? What kind of job is anyone going to get studying history? What kind of living can you make as an author? In Gladwell's case, a spectacularly rewarding brilliant highly acclaimed career with international recognition and almost unlimited financial security!

Why should a business leader study history and read *The Brother's Karamazov*? So they don't wreck themselves and their company.

IBM was run badly starting in the late 1970's, but nobody knew it. Frank Cary, the CEO at the time started to lie, or you might just call it an exaggeration, about IBM's future. He righteously believed that IBM was unstoppable. In a June 13th, 1983 Fortune Magazine article titled "Meet the Lean, Mean, New IBM"...

> *Competitors have felt the ground tremble...their nemesis from Armonk has revolutionized the way it does business, from grand strategy, to the finest tactical detail. 'The company is running on all 16 cylinders,' former DuPont chairman, Irving*

Shapiro, and IBM director, quoted...'There are no limits to its aspirations.'

Sounds impressive. What was the truth? From a publication called the Annex Bulletin (93-07, Jan 1993) and their article entitled *Akers: A Nice Guy Who Lost His Compass...*

By the time (John) Akers became the IBM chairman (in 1985), this was not a time for a 'slick salesman;' it was a time for a 'corporate wrecker,' who would quickly dismantle the unrealistic wishful thinking which envisaged a $180 billion corporation by 1995, conceived by Frank Cary and/or John Opel, the two former IBM CEOs who set the 'Big Blue' on this disastrous course.

What do we call a corporate wrecker? An Iconoclast!

Why was Big Blue blue? There wasn't unlimited demand for their products that existed into perpetuity. They couldn't continue to operate with the same old product using the same old business model. First, they couldn't compete with the mid range products with DEC and their VAX combined with a superior Unix based operating system. Next their mainframe rental contracts started to dry up, so they eliminated their lucrative rental business and started to sell their mainframes to its customer base. A great short term solution to generate cash for a quarter or two but what then?

As Thomas Watson Jr. (the son of the founder Thomas Watson Sr.) Said.

Rental contracts wedded us to our customers, gave us a powerful incentive to keep the service top-notch, and made IBM stable and essentially depression-proof. Once the stream of rental payments dried up, IBM became far more volatile and vulnerable to fluctuations in demand.

Cary and Opel were not leaders; they where righteous opportunists. They righteously made decisions to make the company financials look good until they could get out of town; just like a *snake oil salesman*; just like John D. Rockefeller's father William Rockefeller. John Akers was left holding the bag and looking like a fool. It's a game about deceits and lies and it is a game described in detail and in horror in the book I held in my hand: *The Brothers Karamazov*.

The Brothers Karamazov was to be part of an even more epic story by Fyodor Dostoevsky, called *The Life of a Great Sinner*. And sadly, for too many CEOs, that makes a perfect epitaph. In order to be a CEO and build a sustainable business you have to be a good person. If you read the *Brothers Karamazov* you will discover just how difficult it is for any of us to be good people, especially when we are exposed to great wealth and great power. That is why anyone in a leadership position is obligated to understand what it takes to be a good person; it is why they need to read *The Brothers Karamazov*.

Just to give you a taste, consider what the character Father Zosima, a spiritual advisor says:

Above all, do not lie to yourself. A man who lies to himself and listens to his own lie comes to a point where he does not discern any truth either in himself or anywhere around him, and thus falls into disrespect towards himself and others. Not respecting anyone, he ceases to love, and having no love, he gives himself up to the passions and pleasures, in order to occupy and amuse himself, and in his vices reaches complete bestiality, and it all comes from lying continually to others and to himself.

That is enough to wake anybody up. Does this remind you of anyone? How about former Tyco CEO Dennis Kazlowski throwing lavish decadent birthday parties on the Island of Sardinia? Do you still want to lie to your kids to protect them from making wrong decisions?

Iconoclasts are valuable. Companies like DEC would still be around today if they had an Iconoclast. IBM survived, because they eventually hired a corporate wrecker—an Iconoclast— Louis V. Gerstner.

Ok, so you need an Iconoclast in your company. What do they look like and where are they? They are likely right under your nose, but you have to know what you are looking for. Malcolm Gladwell is an author and Iconoclast. Google him and watch his talks on YouTube. Look in the index of any of his books and you will see the names of other Iconoclasts. Read his books and you will learn how an Iconoclast thinks and how they see and interact with the world.

For example, one fascinating story Gladwell presents is about Howard Maskowitz. Prego hired Howard so he could tell them how to make the best, most perfect spaghetti sauce because they just couldn't gain market share over their competitor, Ragu. Prego felt entitled, because they knew their sauce was better, based on the opinion of experts in the culinary arts. What they wanted to know was how to make an even more perfect sauce. They felt that accomplishing this would restore order to the universe: they would have more market share than Ragu.

Howard ignored what the culinary experts said and instead focused on what people wanted to eat. He wanted to proceed with no assumptions and an open, curious mind using the process of collecting and analyzing data. He went around the country and had people taste different sauces, and had them rate what they liked. When he analyzed the data, it didn't make sense. The data was all over the place. A righteous, perfectionist jerk would just walk away from a study like this and say, "This is wrong, because I knew what the right answer was to begin with. Studies, statistics, analysis don't work. The world is just too complicated. I should continue to operate unchallenged using *my precious* opinions." And that is what righteous people do.

They do not want to appear ignorant or foolish. They do not like their delicate world, constructed largely from their own imaginative lies, tipped upside down and exposed. By contrast, an Iconoclast will be able to see what is in the data, because they have an open mind where they have no fear about discovering the truth.

Howard told Prego that the whole idea of a perfect sauce was an impossible fantasy. The data clustered around specific preferences people had. For example, some people liked their sauce plain and some liked it spicy. What came next was even more astonishing for Prego. There was a huge population of people that loved an extra chunky sauce, where nobody was providing a product, because spaghetti sauce wasn't supposed to be that way.

Despite their fears, Prego did the wrong thing and did what the data suggested; they made the extra chunky sauce. The result? They made 600 million dollars in ten years on this one sauce. They completely distanced themselves from Ragu. What they discovered changed the game permanently for all commercial food products.

What about baseball? What happened when a game that hadn't changed for decades allowed an Iconoclast in? Boston won its first world series! Bill James, a former security guard at Van Camp, and a naturally gifted statistician, analyzed baseball data. And what he discovered was that all conventional thinking was wrong.

One of Bill's realizations was that a player's batting average meant little by itself. Batting average is just a small percentage of a player's total offensive production. Offensive production is the number of bases a player touches. James created something called a "secondary average," which includes walks, extra base hits, and stolen bases. This revolutionized how baseball teams were built, trained and managed! It was this kind of lateral thinking and innovation that allowed Boston to win its first World Series in almost 90 years. Bill James' way of looking at baseball using data and statistical analysis with the open mind of an Iconoclast changed the game.

Typically, the inside expert is unable to challenge his own righteous dogmatic beliefs. As a result, a company becomes rigidly stuck. It sees no way out of the increasingly competitive game it's in, as business steadily declines. That is why the intelligent observations and thinking done by the outside Iconoclast are so incredibly valuable. In fact, the Iconoclast doesn't need to be a subject matter expert in order to make a valuable contribution.

At Shipley, I was assigned to a group that was trying to develop something called a photoimageable soldermask for the printed circuit board industry. Everyone else in the group was either a Ph.D. chemist or a very experienced formulator. I knew nothing. What value could I bring to the table?

In our cloistered area, everyone sat in different cubicles; nobody talked to each other. I spent my day going from cubicle to cubicle asking "stupid" questions and then sitting back, listening and observing. They carefully explained to me why their formulation was the best. Each one of them felt he or she understood how each component behaved. Each one of them believed he or she could predict what would happen when you mixed up stuff; how it would perform at the customer in their process; what the final attributes of the coating would be for the customer's customer.

All these expert formulators were convinced that their *my precious* righteous opinions were perfect. They were outraged when their viewpoint was challenged! So I didn't bother. But they couldn't resist challenging each other. Like a bunch of pack dogs vying for the alpha dog position, these arguments would get ugly. You would hear, "I went to MIT," or "I worked for Cieba

Giegy," or "I worked with the founder of the company, Charlie Shipley."

In order to make "better" formulations they began adding more ingredients! Some of these formulations were pushing almost 25 or more different ingredients! Performance of these new coatings were exponentially worse! The whole project was on a very bad trajectory.

I knew something else needed to be done. "There has got to be a better way," I said to a lady named June McClean.

"There is, Gray," she said. "Did you ever hear of a mixture experiment?"

As she explained it to me, I was reminded of my chemical engineering days, when I learned about mapping mixtures. I asked some of the chemists how they tested their formulations to determine what the levels of the ingredients should be. When I plotted out the different levels and mapped out the concentrations, I discovered they had used the same concentration of ingredients over and over again. They weren't testing different concentration levels, but the exact same formulation where the difference was whether it came from a 1 gallon bucket or a 10 gallon bucket!

As silly as this may sound, it is very easy to do with mixtures. If you add more epoxy, more solvent, more adhesive, and more this and that—thinking more is better—you just get more of what you already had.

June and I set out to design a mixture experiment. We stripped the formulation down to the basic ingredients. Then we looked at changing a couple of ingredients, like a different solvent, or a different type of epoxy. These are known as categorical variables. Then we picked an interesting additive ingredient to include in the study—one that only one of the chemists was using. The net result was we had only five different ingredients in a given formulation, instead of 25 or more different ingredients. From just these five ingredients we were able to come up with many different formulations to study, because we were truly looking at widely different concentration levels.

Since nobody wanted to participate in this study, which was deemed by the experts in the cubes to be a complete waste of time, I alone had to do the lab work. My technique wasn't good. Stuff went flying all over, and sometimes landed on expensive equipment. I often walked out with green chemicals all over me. However, in spite of my poor laboratory technique, what emerged were widely differing responses, one of which became extremely patentable.

That one lucky ingredient that June and I picked, the ingredient that only one chemist used in his formulation, produced what all of us had thought was impossible. I will get back to that in a minute. There is another important story I need to share first: where did this ingredient come from? At that time Shipley R&D was run by a righteous VP that Shipley had hired (see Chapter 3). Charlie Shipley, the cofounder of the company, organizationally reported (dotted line) to this man.

What drove the VP crazy was he couldn't control Charlie. I thought it was strange that he would want to. Charlie was, by definition, the ultimate maverick. Charlie was by all definitions an Iconoclast. The company he started with his wife, Lucia, who operationally made the company work, was entirely Iconoclastic. Someone from academia, like the VP, typically wants to banish or isolate the Iconoclast. Iconoclasts are just too unpredictable. They won't follow methodology, convention, or the rules. Inevitably an Iconoclast is going to do what they want, period. Since the VP couldn't control Charlie he did the next best thing and that was steer everyone else clear of him.

The VP tried all the tactics in his bag of tricks. For example, my manager told me, more or less, "Charlie doesn't know anything about chemistry." Or, "He will lead you on a wild goose chase and ruin you." Or, "If you help Charlie even once you will forever be his slave." Stuff like that. [You will learn about *Ad hominem* in Chapter 12, where you try to weaken a person's credibility to gain a political advantage.]

I don't think Charlie cared. Why would he? When I went to my humble cube in the facility at Newton Lower Falls, an eclectic facility he designed within the walls of an old mill, I walked down a submarine-like hallway past Charlie's office and his stuffed lab. Several times I caught him popping out of his lab with a test tube in his hand holding it to a light outside his door. Charlie seemed to me at these times to be as enthusiastic as a 22 year old college graduate working in his first industrial laboratory!

To the chagrin of the VP, Charlie still secretly communicated and collaborated with many of the older chemists who had been with the company, almost since the beginning. June and I knew, based on our discussions with one of these chemists, that Charlie really thought this substance, which was structurally a very beautiful and complex molecule, was something to look at. Goes to show, you need to listen to your Iconoclast even if you think they are too old, lack the proper academic credentials, and their name is on the outside of the building.

Typically, when formulating a photoimageable soldermask or photoimageable permanent dielectric, you get trade-offs. It is either easy to expose and develop, difficult to make stick, and not resistant; or it is very difficult to expose and develop, easy to make stick, and very resistant. We had come up with a formulation that was everything with no trade-offs! It was easy to develop, had great adhesion, and excellent thermal, mechanical, and environmental properties. The molecule Charlie liked was responsible for this result, a molecule no other competitor was using. This meant that the optimal formulation derived from the designed experiment was patentable!

Why didn't the chemist working with Charlie (in secret) make the same discovery? The formulations they were working with were too complex, where the other additives masked the beneficial effect. And since concentration levels weren't changed, because he was trying to mix up the perfect formulation, you couldn't determine anything from a test other than, did it work? Righteous perfectionists don't do carefully designed experiments. It's impossible for them. And too many chemists are trained to be *know-it-alls* in school. Sadly, it is a very unproductive tradition where everyone wastes a lot of time intellectually beating each other up in a never ending game of one-upmanship.

June and I wrote a paper which I presented at the 1990 BBN Software World Wide Users group meeting in Boston. The designed experiment, or DOE, told us what combination of ingredients and at what concentration these ingredients produced the most beneficial effects across all of the desired characteristics and outcomes. The data driven approach where all sacred cows were challenged was identical in spirit and execution to what Howard Maskowitz did at Prego and what Bill James did at Boston for the Red Sox. Iconoclasts are valuable, but they can create a lot of stress on a manager who wishes tranquillity.

Shortly after completing this work, my boss told me I was being removed from his department. "We're going to see how you do out in the field as a technical service representative," he said. "You are going off to Tokyo and then Taiwan to answer the questions that Nanya, a large company, has asked. Gray, these are the types of questions you like, so make them happy. Good luck."

I happily and naively accepted not realizing I was being sent to my doom—I was being sent on Mission Impossible!

I missed my original flight and arrived in Tokyo's Narita Airport a couple of days late. Nobody met me at the airport. The people who were supposed to pick me up were upset because they didn't know I had missed my flight and had spent the entire night and part of the next morning looking for me. Things were not starting out well.

Thursday morning, still somewhat groggy from my flight, I walked to Shipley headquarters in Tokyo. I went to a small, crowded office where I was told I was expected to create a presentation that would prove to Nanya they would never produce a single defective part if they used Shipley products.

"What?" I said.

"We have already started making the slides," they continued.

I like opportunities in which I can minimize or eliminate risk and gain in all other circumstances. In other words, if the worst happens I lose very little and in all other circumstances I win. However, in this situation, it seemed that whatever move I made I would lose big. Somehow I had been chosen to be crucified for the good of the company. There was no way out! I was briefly paranoid, thinking my old boss was extracting revenge for the damage I did in his lab!

Nanya wanted all of Motorola's business. At the time, a big supplier for Motorola had to conform to their Six Sigma quality initiative and they had to conform to a specific metric called Cpk. To understand Cpk, think about how wide a road needs to be for your tires to stay on it. A Cpk of 1 means the road is only as wide as your tires. With a road that narrow, it won't be long before you drive off the road. A Cpk of 0.5 means two tires will be on the road and two will be off the road all the time. Many production processes operate this way! They have to spend a lot of time and money sorting out the good product from the bad product. Yes, this is extremely inefficient and wasteful.

Conversely, a Cpk of 2 means the road is so wide it might take a billion years before the car drives off. As you might expect, Cpks of 2 are very rare. Nanya wanted to tell Motorola that the Cpk of their processes was 2. And Shipley believed that Nanya wanted to hear that if they used Shipley products they would enjoy a Cpk of 2!

I was assigned to tell them yes, because if I didn't say yes, we wouldn't get the business. What I found interesting was our competitor had already said yes, and Nanya still hadn't given them the business.

I thought I could offer Nanya something totally different. If I was wrong I'd lose my job, but if I was right I'd be a hero, at least to myself. This gave me the confidence I needed to stand up for something important—the truth. Nanya needed to hear the truth. When you stand for something, decisions become easy.

"No!" Would be my answer to Nanya.

So, I started to work. People encouraged me, thinking I was going to tell Nanya what it wanted to hear, "Yes!"

One night I was working late and had enough. It was midnight and I wanted pizza. The head of the Tokyo office was with me and because the boss was there, all of the junior people were there too.

I stopped working and declared, "I am done, unless I get pizza!"

There were giggles from the junior employees who would never think of challenging their boss this way. About 15 minutes later a delivery person dressed in a body suit and uniform, with a hat perfectly placed on his head and the Dominos label precisely stitched on his chest, ran up, handed me the pizza, thanked me in Japanese, and swiftly left. I opened the box and saw a perfectly round pizza, with a grayish, fishy looking cheese over it. It didn't look very appetizing, but was perfectly coated. On each of the four small, perfectly cut pieces was a perfectly placed, single, piece of pepperoni. I stared at this pizza trying to decide what it was. There was absolutely nothing perfect about the perfect placement of the pepperoni! Pizzas aren't supposed to look like this at all! And then it dawned on me. Everyone thinks they know what the perfect presentation is supposed to be, just like the Domino's in Tokyo thinks they know what the perfect pizza is supposed to be. They don't. This made me feel much better about the decision I had made to say, "No." With that, I ate up this thing that was definitely not a pizza.

When I arrived in Taipei, where the Nanya presentation was to take place, the Shipley sales representatives were horrified by what I planned to present. For three straight days, I practiced amidst commands to, "Stop, this will not do."

It became a battle of wills. I would present. They would get upset and then question and intimidate me. Then I would intimidate them back and we would repeat the process.

The day of my presentation I was unconcerned, but everyone else was fidgeting and nervous. There were two conditions made prior to the meeting. First, nobody would leave the meeting until all the presentations were done. Second, Mandarin wouldn't be spoken in order for everyone to understand the conversations. The Nanya conference room was narrow, dimly lit, and crowded. The general manager sat at the head of the table looking stern. He didn't smile; he just looked at me with a laser focus.

I started showing examples, presenting data, and explaining methodology. About 40 minutes in, the boss stared at me intently and asked, "If we use your chemistry can you guarantee we will achieve a Cpk of 2?"

There was a long pause. The room was silent except for the fan from the 3M light projector. With total calm, I looked straight into his eyes and said, "No, Shipley will never guarantee that you will achieve a Cpk of 2. We have a hard enough time trying to achieve such a thing in our own processes. If we were to guarantee such a thing for our customers we would go bankrupt."

I continued to stare right into the eyes of the boss and said, "I can show your people at your factory how to do it, but there are no guarantees," I continued. "You must understand, a Cpk of 2 is a very difficult thing to achieve."

The Shipley representatives of Taiwan and Japan had their heads down in shame. They weren't mad at me, but at themselves for allowing me to speak to such a significant prospect. A prospect that was no more, because I had said "No."

When I completed my presentation, most of the Nanya people left the room in a flash! The first agreed-upon rule had been broken. So much for rules! They reassembled in a room down the hall where they immediately began to confer in Mandarin. From time to time my new, but shamed, friends from Shipley, Far East, would hear, "A Cpk of 2 is very difficult to achieve," in English.

I remained in the dimly-lit conference room listening to a colleague present to the two very young Nanya engineers who had been left behind. Afterwards, I was driven to the airport by a Shipley sales representative. The mood was funereal.

Back in the States, I was called into my boss's office. Apparently, word was already filtering back about the outstanding job I did! Nanya wanted to know how soon I could fly out again! Shipley had gotten the contract.

Later, at a celebratory dinner, Nanya's vice president of operations said, "Gray, you are like a rock. You don't do the right thing. You do what is right." Remembering *The Brothers Karamazov* and the long hours and days it took me to read the thing, I knew what that meant. I try to tell the truth as best I can and if I don't know what the truth is I launch an investigation and proceed carefully with an open mind.

Anyway, this was very nice to hear. It's also the reason why my consulting company is named Grayrock. I like that name, because I believe it symbolizes what an Iconoclast is. An Iconoclast may appear to be stubborn, but what they are doing is holding to what they believe to be true, based on much thought, study, and research. They will change their opinion if observation and measurement proves their position false, but they will not be persuaded by someone's over-confident, righteous opinion. Like a rock, Iconoclasts break old ideas, because that is what the learning *process* is all about. Unfortunately, this upsets righteous people.

CHAPTER 10 SUMMARY

Righteous people like to label and if you are standing up for what is right—for the truth—don't be surprised if you are labelled an Iconoclast. When companies are struggling and not growing they blame all sorts of outside circumstances, but the real problem is they need a fresh look. They need new ideas. They need an intelligent outsider, an Iconoclast, who will tell them the truth; they need an outsider who brings a counter culture perspective that completely goes against the existing righteous, dogmatic beliefs.

Does this work? Is the Iconoclast just a nuisance to be ignored or someone extremely valuable? Because of an Iconoclast, Prego was able to make a wrong, chunky sauce, which earned them 600 million dollars. Because of an Iconoclast, the Boston Red Sox were able to win the World Series by realizing that batting averages meant next to nothing. By ignoring all of the dogmatic beliefs of *expert* formulators with decades more experience than me, I was able to discover a chemical formulation that exceeded what was thought possible. When I ignored what everyone wanted me to do, and committed what should have been professional suicide, my employer earned a huge contract. The answers that will create the breakthrough solutions you need are always outside of conventional thinking. Yes, their presence is disruptive and stressful, but the Iconoclast is extremely valuable to any business.

WHAT WOULD BE GOOD ABOUT BEING AN ICONOCLAST?

Instructions: What we find when working with new clients is they reject ideas that are outside their sphere of experience, and outside their industry's conventional thinking. This proves to be very limiting and often puts a company on a path of decline. In order to decide whether being an Iconoclast is a good thing or a bad thing, you need to consider, without any bias or negativity, all of the possible good things that would happen with the Iconoclast. Use your partner with this exercise.

By being an Iconoclast or working with an Iconoclast you would find... (consider the question)?

1= Meaningless 2= OK 3= Some Benefit 4= Big Benefits 5= Life Changing

➤ The Ability to transform your business in an unforeseen way that your competition can't anticipate, would be?

1	2	3	4	5

➤ Having an outside intelligent force makes you completely rethink every facet of your business would be?

1	2	3	4	5

➤ Excited employees that want to dedicate themselves to the new way would be?

1   2   3   4   5

➤ Coming up with real breakthrough solutions where your competitors are no longer a threat would be?

1   2   3   4   5

➤ Anxiety and pressure lifted, because the company is moving and flowing in a very positive direction would be?

1   2   3   4   5

➤ Accomplishing what was thought to be impossible, would be?

1   2   3   4   5

➤ By just flipping what everybody thinks is wrong and testing it to see if it is in fact right would be?

1   2   3   4   5

➤ Knowing you can take your Iconoclast view and use it for any problem, whether you have experience or not would be?

1   2   3   4   5

➤ Many people may not understand you but they would trust you and your creative mind would be?

1   2   3   4   5

➤ Being able to know that you will always be highly valued by any company would be?

1   2   3   4   5

19 or below

We will never be close friends!

20 to 39

You see a significant opportunity in being an Iconoclast or in hiring an Iconoclast. Now that you see the possibility, how are you going to manifest this into reality? If you want to be an Iconoclast, try to identify if your company is stuck in a rut. Start by assuming every single assumption is wrong. Then experiment and test and see what you discover. If you can do this you are well on your way to being an Iconoclast who is making valuable discoveries.

40 or Above

Good for you! A bright future is in front of you. That is provided the rest of the company isn't scored high in the first five chapters for DAM thinking. If this is the case then you should go find a better company where your unconventional viewpoint will be appreciated.

CHAPTER 11

Tell Them You Are Incompetent

The best defense is a good offense.

—Vince Lombardi

In the movie U-571, a US Navy first mate becomes captain of his crew, which is trying to navigate a German U boat. They can't even read the dials and valves, because everything is in German. After one mishap after another, the submarine, with its skeleton crew rests at the bottom of the ocean. The rookie captain basically tells everyone the truth: "I don't know what to do." As he continues, he is basically telling the crew that he is incompetent. Later, the master chief asks, "Permission to speak freely." He then proceeds to lambast the captain, saying, "Don't you ever say to a crew you don't know what you are doing! You are the captain!" Essentially telling the captain to *fake it before you make it*. Somehow the captain singularly figures out how to get out of their completely impossible situation. They not only get out of it, but they sink an enemy destroyer, with one torpedo! This is Hollywood. This is not an example of how to run your company.

Let me contrast this with a real story. At a local restaurant where I know the staff, they started a new crew of executive chefs. The old ones had been fired a few days prior. Like the new submarine captain, they didn't know what they were doing. And like the master chief, mistakenly did, they told the crew at the restaurant that they knew what they were doing and didn't need any help. Within a short period of time, meals that would normally come out in 10 to 15 minutes were coming out in 45 minutes to an hour. Some of the staff were saying, "If they would just ask for help this wouldn't be such a disaster." This is the real world, with people pretending they have the answers, that they are perfect, who won't ask for help when they need it. That is why declaring incompetence is the perfect foil for employees who do damage to companies: they feel they have to pretend they know what they are doing.

A lot of coarse language is bandied about by people in business. But one word is considered forbidden. It should only be uttered after careful consideration. It is the word *incompetent*.

I, however, embrace this word. Many times, at many plants, I have walked with a customer and observed a process. I have listened and observed. Eventually, an operator has come up to me and said, "You probably know this already…" and then started to explain something, worried that I would react negatively to his suggestion.

I would stop him and say, "Look, I may look smart, but let me tell you a secret. I am incompetent. There is nothing you are going to tell me that will insult my intelligence."

He would look at me for a minute with a puzzled expression on his face. Is this guy serious?

Then he would break into a big smile, and share everything with me—every little detail. I would sit there, soak it all up and learn a lot about how operators, workers, engineers, etc., view their environment, work and contribution.

Had I said, "Yes, you are insulting my intelligence because I am perfect," this rich exchange of information would never happen. Some people find admitting incompetence is a risky, even dangerous, thing to do. I came to the conclusion that it is only risky if you are truly ignorant and unwilling to learn. When you don't listen to others, you have a DAM problem.

Over the years I have run across many former General Electric employees. They are typically very smart and come from the best schools: Notre Dame, Harvard, or Purdue, for example. To a certain extent you have to be aggressive to be hired, work, and survive at GE. Many friends who have worked there tell me "if you make a mistake at GE, your career is done."

GE's culture demands perfection, and many companies hire former GE employees. AlliedSignal was one such company. Larry Bossidy, the CEO of AlliedSignal at the time I worked there, was a former GE employee.

At AlliedSignal, the most efficient meetings I attended were run by former GE employees. But there was a problem. When there was a risky decision to be made, a decision that required lateral thinking (a natural way of thinking for an iconoclast) things ground to a halt. The former GE employees wanted to make the perfect decision every time.

I've always wondered why some high-growth companies suddenly slowed down and became low growth. Is it because they hired too many perfectionists? Growth absolutely demands taking risks and moving with high velocity. This is the nature of a FLOW thinking company. With FLOW you cannot know, absolutely, what is going to happen. Unexpected things will emerge. They may be good or they may be bad. This isn't a judgment, it is fact. FLOW thinkers learn to improvise and sometimes they are wrong. Because of this, they are sometimes seen by perfectionists (who have no tolerance for mistakes) as being incompetent.

I sometimes wonder why some companies have such a tough time selecting a CEO. Most companies hire the CEO from the outside. Why? My conclusion is that insiders, having made mistakes, are considered by their company's board of directors to be incompetent. The outsider has the advantage of hiding his or her mistakes and painting a perfect picture.

CEO candidates rarely start their interview by saying, "Hi, I just wanted to let you know that I get good results not because of what I do, but because of the outstanding people who work for me. I am actually incompetent." Instead, they try to project an image of perfection. Why wouldn't they? That is exactly what most companies want. Few companies look into the behaviors and the thinking of their CEO candidates because many boards of directors don't understand that work is social, behaviors lead results, and our behaviors are governed by our thinking.

One company I know hired a new CEO and placed him in an office where there was a lot of people traffic. It was the perfect place for a leader who believed, "work is social" and wanted to encourage communication, develop trust, and be in the know. However, the new CEO soon vacated this office and moved to the other side of the building, as far away from his employees as he possibly could. Because of this, the CEO was constantly surprised by the company's never ending string of crises.

Why did he hide on the other side of the building? Perhaps he didn't want people to know he wasn't perfect. Perhaps he was afraid that others would view him incompetent. This CEO had a lot of thinking DAMs, DAMS which could have (and should have) been recognized during the interview and selection process. With this CEO, the company now had a DAM problem.

The last thing a successful CEO wants is to be isolated, to operate on a little island. Making decisions in isolation increases the probability of making bad decisions (like the sinking of my Jeep) which is why a mastermind is much more intelligent than a single, smart mind. But CEOs aren't encouraged to collaborate. They came to their position by proving they are better than others—Ego DAM. The have shown that they always have the right answer from their vast well of experience and knowledge—Learning DAM. Collaboration in almost any company today does not get you promoted. And that is why I believe there are so many mediocre and bad CEOs. They are a product of a system that encourages isolation and individual contribution and maximizes DAM thinking.

What do companies score? It isn't the success or the size of the success that drives this system but whether you are fallible or not. Did you make a mistake? If you did there must be something wrong with you. What does the aspiring CEO do? Blame someone else of course. Fail to take any accountability. When the Deepwater Horizon blew up in the Gulf of Mexico, did Tony Hayward, the CEO of British Petroleum at the time, take any accountability? No. Why? In order to get the CEO job in a large fortune 500 company you have to be perfect. To keep the job you have to be perfect. If something goes wrong you are still perfect, because it was someone else's fault. Could you imagine what the world of business would be like if you could make a mistake, learn from it, and still be promoted to the top job?

The best CEOs surround themselves with talented teams. They put those teams in the middle of the action. Here's what Mike Myatt says about this in *The CEO Survival Manual*:

> *"Great CEOs surround themselves with tier-one talent and the best advisors money can buy. They don't make uninformed or ill-advised decisions in a vacuum."*

And on his website—*Management Matters*—Myatt states:

> *"By exhibiting strong leadership skills a good CEO will manage talent, performance, change, innovation, influence, rapport, and messaging to consistently drive an enterprise forward regardless of circumstances."*

Great CEOs can't hide in a corner. They have to deal with the fact that not only are they not perfect but, in one or more areas required for the job, they may actually be incompetent. They can survive only if they have a strong team. Work is social. Isolated CEOs fail.

Kenneth Iverson made Nucor Steel a great company. In his book *Good to Great*, Jim Collins made this point:

> *"Iverson's assistant tells of a scene repeated...colleagues would march into Iverson's office and yell and scream at each other, but then emerge with a conclusion. Argue and debate, then sell the nuclear business; argue and debate, then focus on steel joists; argue and debate, then begin to manufacture their own steel, ... the company's strategy, evolved through many agonizing arguments and fights."*

In many companies it is considered a disaster for people to argue and debate with intensity. At best, such behavior is considered unprofessional. More often it is judged to be a failure of the business. Yet at Nucor, out of these very imperfect meetings a most wonderful company emerged! Today, Nucor is considered to be one of the dominant steel companies in the world and it became so by allowing its people to argue and be perfectly unprofessional.

When we are allowed to argue, we have more freedom to speak the truth as we see it. And through this communication, if we do it well, we can understand other facets of the issue by listening to others' arguments. When we aren't allowed to argue we are faced with a dilemma. Do we do the right thing and break rules and be outcast or fired or do we do the *perceived* right thing and just go along knowing we are contributing to the problem and possibly the demise of the business? When we aren't allowed to argue then the business results will declare our incompetence.

There are two things that we have a hard time doing that really hold us back from flowing and growing. First, we all have a real hard time doing the right thing when everyone wants us to do the wrong thing. Second, it's really difficult for any of us to admit we don't know what we are doing and ask for help. What do successful people do?

People have told me they found my first book, *Change Your DAM Thinking,* inspiring. I asked why.

A common comment was something like this: "You've made so many mistakes in your career, some of them monumental, and yet you seem to be enjoying life and doing quite well. It's a relief to know you don't have to be perfect to succeed."

I was caught off guard when I first heard this. I didn't think there were many mistakes I wrote about in my book. And then it dawned on me what was going on and how I have come to see the world as a FLOW thinker.

For a FLOW thinker mistakes are just bumps in the road and for a DAM thinker mistakes are the end of the road.

DAM thinkers are terrified of being found out as being incompetent. They are terrified to negotiate for raising their prices, or change the customer payment policies, or install a new computer system, or launch an unknown product to market, or implement a program to improve customer service, or lower the inventory level of their plant, or set standards and make their employees accountable. DAM thinkers fear making changes that might go wrong, and could be blamed on them. Instead of moving forward, there is one delay after the next. We need to wait because later things will be better and more perfect. We need to wait because we will have better information. We need to wait because not to have a perfect outcome would be devastating. We need to wait so we don't take the wrong actions that could expose us as incompetent.

Why is it so horrible to admit incompetence and ask for help? When we pretend to be the hero in the movies and pretend we know what we are doing, when we don't, is when we plunge our company into real trouble.

I remember going to Tempe, Arizona to visit a high density, printed circuit board shop. I was hired to do an evaluation. People were expecting me to spend a day or two there to determine what was wrong. They were expecting a highly detailed report with numbers, figures, and tables. And they expected my report to take over a month to put together. I remember walking into the lobby that was packed with junk. The plant manager popped his head out and invited me into his office, which was packed with junk. He immediately started to explain his woes. How his plant would be perfect if he was just allowed to run it without interference; if he was his own boss, not part of another corporation, where he had unlimited funds, everything would be perfect. If he had this then he wouldn't have any problems.

He then escorted me to another messy office, to the manufacturing supervisor of the plant. At this point, 15 minutes into my tour, I wanted to leave. I had seen and heard enough. There was so much pollution I just couldn't stand it. And I don't care who you are in a business, if it is polluted, it isn't your boss's fault, or corporate's fault for not approving your capital expenditures, it is your fault! We then proceeded through the plant. There were 55 gallon drums everywhere, broken down pumps, dirty tanks, dirty walls, dirty equipment, it stunk to high Heaven, the air hurt my eyes, the operators looked really unhappy and demoralized, product was sitting everywhere and on everything. It was truly depressing. Nothing was moving. Everything was stagnant. Everyone and everything was under an extreme amount of pressure and money was literally going down the drain.

I asked this manager what was wrong. Again, it was the economy, the customer, the people at corporate. And I asked, "What about here?" His answer? Everything would be perfect if it wasn't for *them*. I asked him, "Do you understand why I am here?" And he answered, "No, because there isn't anything here that is causing a problem. We are perfect." And then he gave me a show-and-tell of different products that they made and why they were the best in the world. Both he and his boss truly believed that.

After he was done, I just left. I was there for only two hours. They immediately called the CEO back at corporate to say, "Why did this guy come down? He just left. He didn't learn anything. He wasted our time." They were unwilling to ask for help. The condition of the entire shop told me they didn't know what they were doing and that they were completely incompetent. The fact that they were unwilling to ask for help told me the team needed to be replaced immediately. The technical problems with the facility were irrelevant. The shop had a serious DAM leadership problem.

Before I left I asked for the routing (the process steps and instructions) for their top job number (the job that they made the most of). Remembering the layout of the plant I translated the steps and overlaid the sequences so that the chaos of the flow wouldn't look like a complete ball of yarn, which it was. I then reorganized the locations of some of the equipment, drew up how information would put starts and stops in the production flow so operations would stay full or wouldn't become overloaded. I included estimates of production rates, lead times, inventory levels, and estimates for improvement on product quality. I had drawn up, visually, how the shop would be organized for FLOW. I wrote a summary document and submitted it to the CEO. He got the report in 48 hours. He had never seen anything like it. Based on the potential demonstrated in the report, it was clear a change in plant leadership needed to be made. When we choose to pretend we are perfectly competent is when we, in fact, prove how completely incompetent we are.

The best defense is a good offense, which I translate: *be offensive and declare your incompetence.*

I remember declaring in a meeting, "I am incompetent." An executive pulled me aside and said, "What are you doing? Are you mad? Do you want to ruin your career?" And I thought, "How am I going to find out the kind of help available to me, help I need in order to accomplish my mission?"

I believe, today, nothing is more powerful for a mission-driven employee than declaring incompetence and asking for help. And it is probably the most valuable thing you can do for your company. This advice applies to all levels, especially the CEO. But you can only get away with this if your request is for real help and you believe in a passionate way or have almost a pathological belief that you will succeed. Without this strong absolute positive belief, declaring your incompetence will get you sacked behind your own goal line.

AlliedSignal Laminate Systems started a pay-for-service business called STEP. It was not the free technical service customers received as part of the sales process. No customer is ever grateful for free service—that is just human nature. STEP was an attempt to create a new paradigm for AlliedSignal and its customers. We worked with our customers on real projects that would advance their position and minimize daily crises by solving real problems. I was to lead the group along with three other very talented people.

I told the team early on that they "may think I know what I am doing, but I don't. I have no clue. I am incompetent in what I have been asked to do here. I have never done it before. No one in our industry has done this before. I don't know what customers to go after first. I don't know what we are going to offer them. I don't know what price we should charge. And that is just the start of what I don't know. We are all going to have to step up if we don't want to go down in flames." They looked confused. Then they realized I wasn't kidding.

Though they were anxious, they immediately became very motivated. Right from the start our meetings were intense. As before, I worked with a friend from GE. He was very smart but he hated argumentative debate.

We were very nice to each other and followed an agenda for the first ten minutes of the first meeting. Then I looked at the person speaking and said more or less, "I can't listen to this anymore and here is why: you didn't consider points X, Y, Z! Furthermore, take this example that happened out at a customer's site…"

And so it went. It became clear we needed more resources to quickly figure out the answers to our business questions. I wasn't happy with how the team was still trying to protect each other's feelings, especially when it came time to make decisions. They seemed to be looking for compromise and consensus, two words that I truly detest.

I called in Frank Delk, a friend from Monsanto days, to observe our meetings and provide some coaching. Frank watched for a while, then interjected, explained ways we could better frame our challenges, problems, and questions. He also showed how we could better appreciate each person's modalities of learning and personality. He would also interject his own ideas and experience suggesting what we might do with the business. What Frank didn't do was lower the level of intensity or conflict in our debates. If anything, they became more intense, but less emotional. My intensity and passion was still way outside the comfort zone of everyone else on the team. Frank filled in some enormous gaps that I had as leader, but he and I were both concerned that the team wasn't pushing back at me strongly enough.

Early on, my teammates started to complain about me to Frank.

The discussion would go something like, "You have to get Gray to change because this isn't working."

Frank knew I wasn't going to change my personality no matter what the situation. He told me my team was complaining but that he would not bring the complaints to me. "It's up to them to do it if they don't like something. I told them to talk to you directly."

In time, my teammates approached me with their internal conflicts and I told them, "I am not going to change. You are just going to have to push back. I am sorry if this is outside your comfort zone."

Finally, they did start to push back; some with brute force, some with great finesse, each different, and each in a style that suited their personality and strengths.

Once this happened, you could instantly see the true people. Instead of polite personalities that didn't feel comfortable speaking freely, each person's true personality came out and the flow of communication accelerated. People became in tune with their feelings and the reasons for the emotional reactions to issues we would discuss. And once they realized that not everyone was going to be happy all of the time, the team started to perform at a much higher level. They understood it was important to figure things out, make good decisions together, and have a spirited debate that dug deep for the truth. For some, this experience changed them. Others fell back to their old ways of doing things after the project came to an end.

STEP was successful right from the start. Our first client liked our services; liked the quick results we delivered, and paid us the full amount invoiced, on time. Surprisingly, this was not good news for some people within AlliedSignal Laminate Systems. The sales people could not understand or explain the difference between free services and STEP services. STEP did not fit with their concept of how their perfectly comfortable world should work. They liked giving their customers free bags of corn, because they thought it entitled their customers to be beholden to them!

As soon as you bundle something and say it is free, because you want the customer to like you, you instantly deflate the value of your work, of your service, of your product. Giving something away never works out. People always want more and more and more. And you rarely receive even one thank you. After all, *no good deed goes unpunished*. Free products and services always command low respect in the eyes of the customer. Many people thought customers wouldn't pay for STEP, but they did! So the company, driven mainly by input from the sales and marketing department, killed it. The sales people were terrified to have to learn a new pattern of securing a customer account. They were very much attracted to the old pattern where they could give away something significant for free.

The STEP experience reinforced the lesson I learned when my sister and I gave away free corn. You will just create entitled people who will not respect you or even say thank you. But that is exactly what many sales people would like. If you were to ask the sales department to quote the perfect price for a product they would likely quote a price lower than the competitors'. If the competitors lowered their price, sales would come back and ask to have the price lowered even more, and so it would go. What STEP proved was that price isn't the only reason customers buy. There are also other reasons. If you don't know what those other reasons are you don't have a sales problem. You have a business problem.

Confess your imperfections and people will be very willing to help you. The longer you try to keep up the façade that you are perfect, the more miserable you will become. If you think you need perfect people, with perfect products, perfectly priced, for perfect customers, you will fail.

CHAPTER 11 SUMMARY

Conceding that you are less than perfect (even occasionally admitting you are incompetent) will draw people to you. They will want to help you. They will want to work with you. Many people in business think there are perfect ways to conduct meetings, perfect ways to talk to each other, and perfect ways to work with each other and make decisions. But when this one-size-fits-all view is pushed on us, it removes diversity and compromises who we are. By sometimes having imperfect meetings that fall apart, we start to see the unique talents that allow a team to function at a high level. We are at our best when we admit our imperfections. Admitting our flaws isn't being defensive, it is just stating the obvious. This allows the others on your team to fill in your gaps as you fill theirs.

What should you do when you encounter perfectionistic behavior or a perfectionist-driven company culture?

People will thank you for helping them get rid of their perfectionistic mindset—the idea that they have to be perfect. They will find pleasure in experiencing less pressure, less stagnation, and less pollution. Striving to be better in an atmosphere of understanding and support is unfortunately all too rare. By attacking the perfectionist behavior in your company you will derive a marked increase in performance with a rise in morale. You will become much more competitive.

As the leader of your business, department, or group, you can define the environment. This will change the behaviors that will lead results. For example, celebrate mistakes when they are made. Explain the context. Explain how this is part of the journey for success.

Get people to admit that they aren't perfect. And bring people together to figure out as a group how to work together.

Accelerate a free and open flow of communication. Send the message that it is impossible to over communicate. Encourage people to share their stories, their mistakes, and their learnings.

In order to remove perfectionist behavior from your company, you don't necessarily have to go to the extreme of admitting incompetence; however. be aware that we all are sometimes incompetent in this highly advanced technological age. That's OK, we can always ask for help, unless of course we have an Ego DAM.

WHAT WOULD BE GOOD ABOUT DECLARING YOUR INCOMPETENCE?

Instructions: There is so much pressure associated with pretending you aren't human, but rather a machine incapable of making mistakes. And then when you do make one, the pressure of trying to figure out how you're going to hide it, or what story you're going to come up with, or who you're going to blame, is extreme. Work with your partner again and see what the potential impact would be in your life by declaring your incompetence.

By admitting you were incompetent you would find...

1 = Meaningless 2 = OK 3 = Some Benefit 4 = Big Benefit 5 = Life Changing

➢ Less pressure because there is no longer any need to blame people or come up with complicated excuses would be?

1   2   3   4   5

➢ You lower people's expectations. When you do perform brilliantly the pleasant surprise would be?

1   2   3   4   5

➢ Less pressure to always have the answer would be?

1   2   3   4   5

➢ People will tell you anything, because they know they make mistakes too would be?

1   2   3   4   5

➢ A great way to interrupt people when they are arguing about who gets the blame would be?

1   2   3   4   5

➢ More ease in relating to people on a human level would be?

1   2   3   4   5

➢ Who can or who will help you would be?

1   2   3   4   5

➢ A new way to quickly motivate a team by declaring your incompetence would be?

1   2   3   4   5

➤ Setting a powerful example for others to follow where they can say anything and not fear being judged would be?

1　　2　　3　　4　　5

➤ A company culture that is more experimental and innovative where people can make mistakes would be?

1　　2　　3　　4　　5

19 or below

Well, good luck being perfect!

21 to 39

You see advantages to admitting you are fallible and human. The question is whether you want to get to the point, like me, and admit incompetence. There are other things you can say that are less offensive. You can say, "I am not familiar with this, please explain." Or you can say, "Please don't worry if I have heard this already or know it already, I am interested in your unedited explanation." Or simply say, "For this production planning system I am going to need help from everyone. The scope is just too large for a single person." And finally you could say, "I really appreciate your ideas and I would like to consult with you on this." Try these out. But if you want to get people's attention, say you're incompetent.

40 or Above

Looks like you are ready to make a change. Read the paragraph above and see if any of those ideas appeal to you. If you are going to declare yourself incompetent, then you have to have total confidence that what you are doing will eventually work out. You are going to have to be a very persistent driver who has a track record of success. At first, when you succeed, people will wonder if you are playing around with them or if you are trying to make them look foolish; especially competitive people who want to step on you for their own advancement. After a while they will learn there is a reason for your madness. It's like a mantra you use to get going, like may dad always saying near the end of a job, "Good enough for government work." At the end of the day, declaring your incompetence and exhibiting high standards and mastery allows others to admit they are imperfect, too, and need help.

CHAPTER 12

Don't Shoot the Messenger!

What this means is we shouldn't abbreviate the truth but rather get a new method of presentation.

—Edward Tufte

There is a big myth that needs to be debunked: *The U.S. can't compete in manufacturing with China and other emerging markets because of labor rates.* The average wage in China is about $1.83 per hour and the average in the U.S. is about $15 per hour. How can anyone possibly compete in such a market?

By blowing open the Ego DAM, we can compete in manufacturing with anyone in the world. Blowing open the Ego DAM always starts with a single question, "Do you know how to make money in your company?"

"It's not possible! I know we made money this quarter!" More than once I have heard business managers say this after looking at their monthly financial reports. These same managers have often told me how well things are going and how no help is needed. They are proud, and rightly so.

Eventually the manager shares his version of the problem, "Corporate is messed up, especially the cost accounting department. Sometimes they tell me I am making money. Other times they tell me I am losing money. How can that be? It doesn't make sense!"

"Do you know how to make money in your business?" I ask.

His surprised response is always, "Of course!" And after a pause, "Why are you asking me that?"

"Because there is nothing wrong with the Cost Accounting Department," I reply. "The problem is you don't know how to make money with your business. That is what this data says. I'm just the messenger. If you choose not to shoot me, I can help you."

This chapter is about breaking the Ego DAM by welcoming and seeking out the truth. The truth is we can all be better and we all need each other's help.

In order to be helped we have to understand what our problem is and that means we have to listen to those who speak the truth, the messenger, and not shoot him or her. Too often the messenger is shot instead—ad hominem. *Ad hominem* means if you can discredit the messenger, you can ignore and discredit what he says, no matter how valid, logical or right he may be. It means the company may be operating under a myth that it wants to preserve—we are good, our products are great, our customers love us. But a myth may not be factual. It may be a lie!

Joseph Campbell said *"Mythology is what we call someone else's religion."*

A religious viewpoint is not meant to change. It is not meant to be challenged. So when your mythology is attacked, it is a natural reaction to blame the messenger, and the easiest way to do that is by discrediting the character of the messenger. *Ad hominem.*

During the Renaissance, the Italian scientist Galileo proved the Earth was not the center of the universe. The Catholic church arrested him, put him up in front of an inquisition and banned all of his books and scientific writings. The church wasn't ready to face the truth. So it attacked the person and not the message. *Ad hominem.*

For six consecutive years, *Fortune Magazine* sermonized that Enron was the most innovative company in the world! Enron was super smart. It had unique systems of analysis. Its profits and growth were and its future prospects were unlimited! But it was all untrue. It was all based on lies.

Eventually, Sharon Watkins, who worked for Kenneth Lay (Enron's CEO at that time), blew the whistle. Enron was nothing more than a Ponzi scheme.

In a memo to K. Lay, Sharon Watkins wrote, *I am incredibly nervous that we will implode in a wave of accounting scandals.* And that's exactly what happened.

What happened to Sharon Watkins after she sent this memo? According to her lawyer, "Watkins was made to feel 'an outcast.'"

Shoot the messenger, ignore the message. *Ad hominem.*

In the 1980's, NASA believed that the space shuttle was safe to fly—so safe, in fact, that they could send regular people, like school teacher Sharon Christa McAuliffe, on shuttle missions.

On January 28th, 1986, the space shuttle Challenger exploded killing all on board including Christa McAuliffe. Yet the myth persisted that the shuttle is safe! Then the space shuttle Columbia came apart over Texas on February 1st, 2003. As was the case with the Challenger disaster, there were people in NASA and sub-contractors who built critical shuttle components who knew the shuttle wasn't safe. In fact, its lack of safety was obvious to Gen. Chuck Yeager, the world famous test pilot, who said, "The shuttle is an experimental aircraft. They blow up."

Why was it so difficult to get NASA to see the true riskiness of any shuttle mission as clearly as Chuck Yeager?

In his book, *What Do You Care What other People Think*, Nobel Prize winner Richard P. Feynman described his experience on the government commission assigned to investigate the Challenger disaster. Feynman was a FLOW thinker, and the first thing he insisted on was finding the truth. He described his approach:

> *It's called a briefing, but it wasn't brief: it was very intense, very fast, and very complete. It's the only way I know to get technical information quickly: you don't just sit there while they go through what they think would be interesting: instead, you ask a lot of questions, you get quick answers, and soon you begin to understand the circumstances and learn just what to ask to get the next piece of information you need.*

Feynman was told his efforts would be fruitless because NASA was proud of its bird. They were proud of its scale, its complicated systems, and the fact you had to be really smart to be part of the program. NASA also assumed you had to be really smart to figure out why it blew up, and even if you did, you had to be even smarter to explain why it blew up.

NASA was a DAM thinking organization. Only a DAM thinking organization can be in a crisis and think everything is just fine. Work is social. Behaviors lead to results. And our behaviors are governed by our thinking.

Within a few weeks, Feynman found the data charted in Figure 2 below. Morton Thiokol, which manufactured the large booster rockets mounted on either side of the shuttle, sent this data up to NASA management prior to launch. The intent was to postpone the launch until the weather was warmer. The temperature on the launch pad at the time the Shuttle launched was 29°F. The previous coldest launch was 53°F.

O Ring Incedents VS °F at Launch

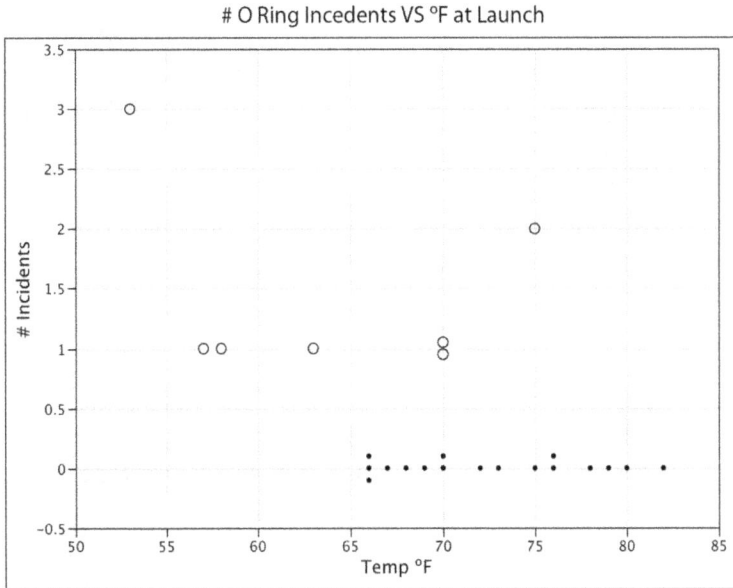

Figure 2:
Data showing don't launch at 29 °F!

Think of each large booster rocket as a stack of gigantic canisters filled with highly explosive toothpaste. Putty and big rubber O-rings were used as seals between these canisters. As the fuel burns, you want the hot flames and heat to be contained in the canister. If there are any leaks, then the huge tank could be ignited. Boom! The data in figure 2 indicates where there was an incident (the hollow circles).

The putty and rubber O-rings were there to prevent leaks from the subsections that were stacked one on top of the other. The O-ring compensates for the compression at launch and the expansion after lift-off. An O-ring incident meant the O-ring was burning, and likely leaking flames and hot gasses!

The data above indicates there were serious problems with the O-rings being able to compress and then expand correctly at cooler temperatures like those during the launch. The trend in the data indicates things got worse as the temperature of the O-ring got colder. But even when the O-ring was warm, there were still incidents. The data indicates that the shuttle wasn't safe at almost any temperature because the O-rings weren't keeping the hot gasses and flames inside of the canister.

Yeager was right! The shuttle wasn't safe. That was the message in the data. A fourth grader could see it. What the data showed was (a) don't launch now and when it warms up (b) still don't launch in fact, (c) never launch the thing ever again. IT'S NOT SAFE.

But they did launch. Why? NASA discredited the data because it indicated that even when you had an O-ring incident, the shuttle didn't blow up. If this reminds you of my Jeep story and a false sense of entitlement, it should. Be daring, defiant, and free was an extremely dangerous mind set for NASA to embrace. The Ego DAM is a large component of entitlement. NASA had a serious Ego DAM. They chose to ignore the data and shot the messenger by discrediting the engineer's interpretation of the data. That alone should have been a warning not to launch! If the engineers didn't know what they were doing, which is what management accused them of, then the answer should have been to delay the launch, because management is not qualified to make complicated engineering decisions concerning the systems and their safety. However the Challenger was launched.

Ad hominem.

If you want your business to blow up, then shoot the messenger by discrediting her. If you want to know how to make money in your business then I have some very direct messages for you. First, *don't shoot the messenger*. Second, read the other messages I have bolded for you below.

CHANGE YOUR DAM BEHAVIOR! YOUR EMPLOYEES AREN'T THE PROBLEM!

Can you measure the bad behaviors of a management team before a crisis like that of the space shuttle happens? Yes, if you are willing to accept that you have two choices: 1) Have a DAM thinking culture or 2) have a FLOW thinking culture. Moreover, understand that if you have a DAM thinking culture in your company you, your people, and your management are going to be burning up resources; you're bad behavior is going to weaken your company's performance. And the chance of having a business crisis is high.

How is it done? Using the five Thinking DAMs, described in this book and my other book, *Change Your DAM Thinking*, and the Six Musts of a FLOW Thinking Company—accountability, skill, standards, commitment, observation, and improvisation—it is very easy to determine the state of an organization, DAM or FLOW, and to predict trouble. Consider the diagram shown in Figure 3.

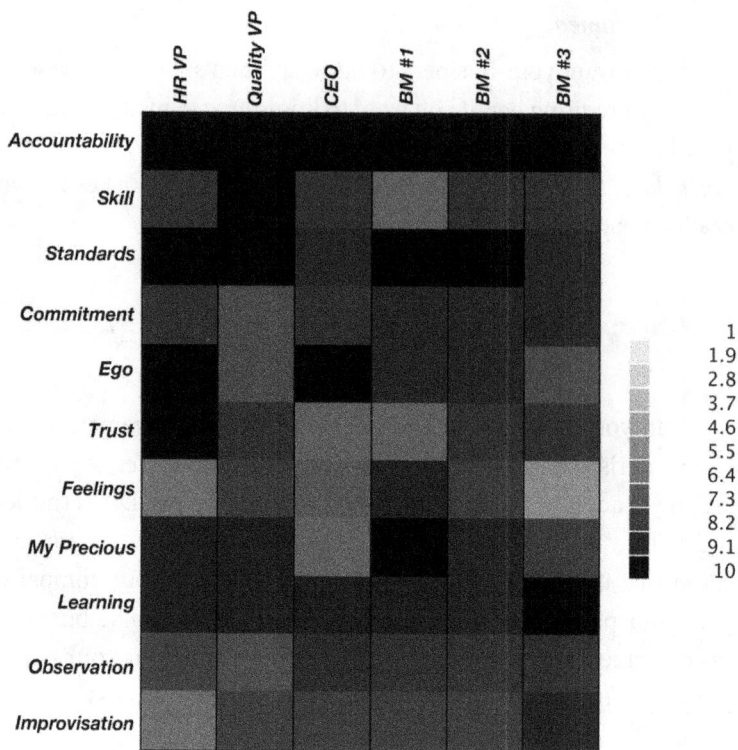

Figure 3:
How each team member thought about themselves.

This chart was for an executive team of a smaller technology company. The darker the square, for example, the dark square on the first row, which is for *Accountability* in the *CEO* column, means the CEO believes she is absolutely accountable, based on her answers to our survey questions. Nobody on this executive team was willing to admit they weren't accountable. Was that the truth? We shall see later! For now, consider this: did the NASA management team that decided to launch think they were accountable for the space shuttle disaster? Did Kenneth Lay think he was accountable for the demise of Enron? It's a recurring theme that when a business is in crisis, leadership thinks they weren't accountable for the crisis. However, if you ask them if they are accountable as people and in their jobs, they will say absolutely!

Let's look at the second row for *Skill*. This would be how each person feels about their skill level and whether they feel they have absolutely all the skill they need to do their job now and in the future. Notice anything? The Quality VP rates himself very high. In chapter 11 we discussed the importance of declaring your incompetence in order to motivate a team and be exposed to as much help as possible. How likely is it that the Quality VP is going to ask for help? Is there an Ego DAM? Or, is there something else going on with this team?

Notice that one business manager (BM #1) admitted that he had a weakness in his skills, and looking at the learning row, he thinks he is open to learning and not a "know-it-all." The light square for skill, according to the legend on the right, is about a 2.8. The lower the number, the less skill people they have. For learning, which is the Learning DAM, a high score of about a 7.3 means this manager didn't think he had much of a Learning DAM. This is a very healthy result for skill for this individual!

Is this a healthy chart for the team? Unfortunately, no, and there are several reasons for this. What you want to see in a good team is high scores for each individual on trust, with some variation in accountability. It may seem strange, but individuals on a dysfunctional team are unwilling to share truthful information to others concerning their behaviors, such as accountability. And since accountability is a big deal for a team's performance, and for pleasing the boss, nobody is going to admit that they have any accountability issues. The only way this can happen in an honest way is for the CEO to admit his own accountability issues, which was discussed in Chapter 11, *Tell Them You Are Incompetent*. The same goes for skills. You would only admit that you have weaknesses in your skill sets with people you trust, and a leader that will allow you to admit your weaknesses in an environment that is safe.

What is really a red flag is that the CEO rated herself low on a Trust DAM. She perceives the need to fully communicate and share information with her closest team to be low. The problem with this is you are either going to trust the team that you have hired or you are not. You can't pick and choose what you are going to share or not share in terms of communication. The fact that the My Precious rating is also low indicates that she feels a need to protect her turf. This, along with the low feelings DAM score, is a very bad sign. This implies a lack of personal security and this bodes trouble for this company. The good news is that 1) the CEO sees a problem in herself and 2) seeing the problem she can be coached through it. Fixing just this can change the dynamics of the executive and the culture of the company very quickly.

There are two more charts that make the problems I indicated above obvious to anyone.

Figure 4 below shows how each individual rated the performance of the team. You may wonder if the individuals were truthful in what they said about themselves. How can you tell if they lied or were not being honest with themselves? Do you see the low ratings for accountability for some members of the team? This means there is a level-of-accountability issue with the team. But nobody is admitting it to themselves, because they think individually they are perfectly accountable. The stories don't match, which means people aren't telling the truth and the likely reason is fear.

Note the CEO doesn't think much of the team's ability to improvise. This is likely accurate. In order to improvise a team absolutely has to be in FLOW and that means no Thinking DAMs, which would show on this diagram as high scores (very dark squares) for Ego, Trust, Feelings, My Precious, and Learning. The CEO thinks there are issues on her team with the Ego DAM: people aren't asking for help when they should; the Trust DAM: people aren't communicating openly and honestly on the team; the Feelings DAM: people are doing things to make others feel good instead of bringing up issues vital to the purpose of the company. Again, the low level of trust that the CEO has for her team is a very bad sign.

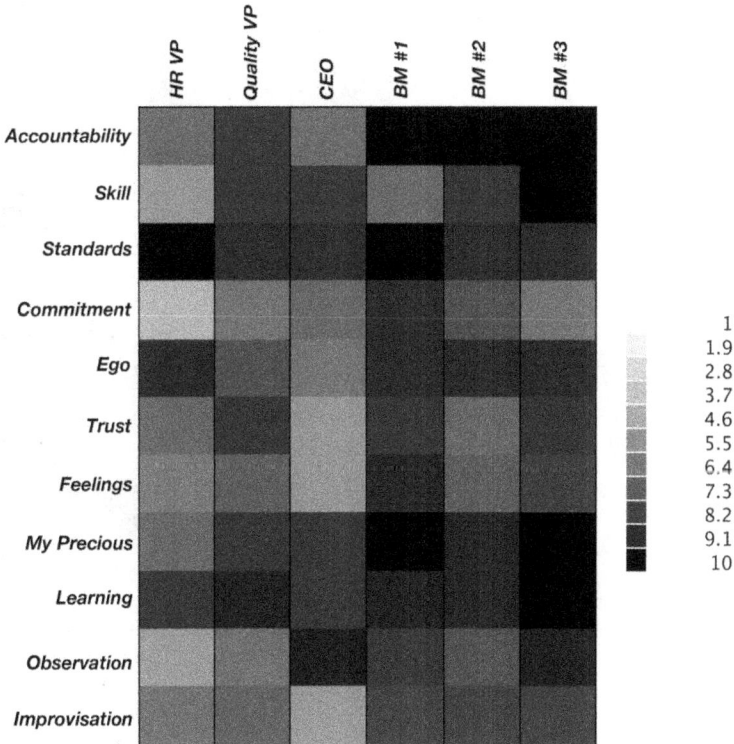

Figure 4:
What each team member thought about the executive team.

You might wonder at this point how bad is it? My interpretation of these charts may not be crystal clear to you. Figure 5 should be more than crystal clear to you.

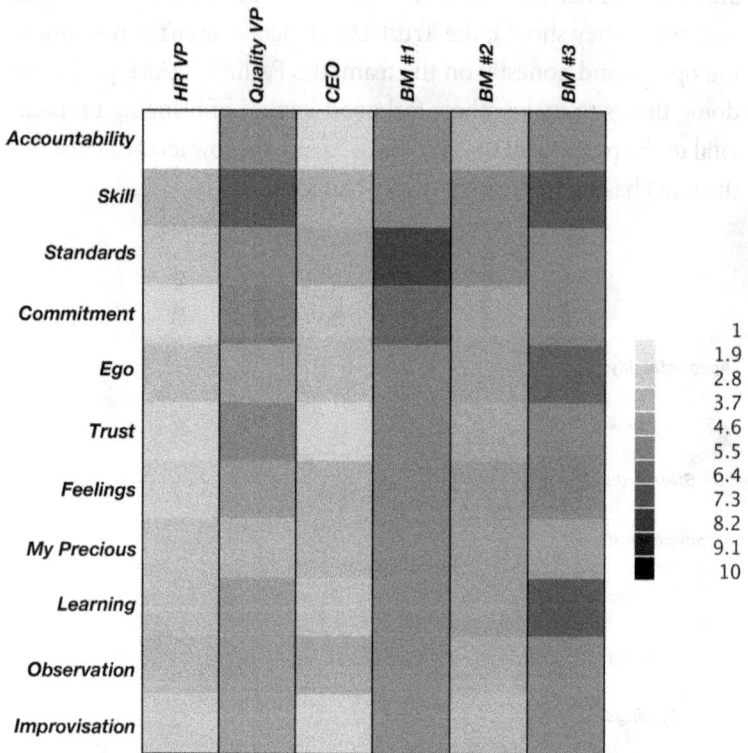

Figure 5:
This is what the executive team thought about all of the employees in the company!

And what is clear about Figure 5 is everyone, other than the team, gave horrible ratings across the board to the employees of the company! This is the one area on which everyone absolutely agrees! This raises some obvious questions. First, who is responsible for hiring the right people for the company? Second, who is responsible for creating the right environment to attract good people? Third, who is taking the blame for performance issues with this company? Finally, what group of people is ultimately accountable for results? Is there a DAM problem with this company? Is it obvious?

This type of result isn't unusual for a DAM thinking company. I remember a CEO friend of mine who walked out of a meeting with a very troubled company. The meeting was very long. He expected each of the executives to present him with an honest assessment of the business. Instead, they told him why they were wonderful and why this team of executives was wonderful, too. He thought, "If these people are so great why is the company tanking? How can this possibly be the fault of all of the employees when they ultimately work for these executives?"

My friend quickly realized he had to do something. His first step was to ignore his team because he couldn't trust them to provide the information he needed. The second step was to go down to the lower level managers and supervisors, listen and observe, discover what the true issues were, and build trust with the work force. His third step was to put the executives in a vice-like grip that set a new standard for honesty. He admitted he didn't trust them and why. He shared what he found out and how it was inconsistent with their stories. He warned them that if they didn't present him with the facts and be honest in their communications that they would be fired. This large company turned around very quickly.

The culture he created was like a freight train of messengers who were allowed to speak and be heard.

CAN YOU HANDLE THE TRUTH? LEARN TO FIND IT AND DEAL WITH IT!

In a culture based on fear—a DAM thinking culture—it is very easy to not tell the truth, and shoot the messenger. Who wants to be the messenger who gets shot? Figure 6 shows, just by simple averaging, how the truth can be buried.

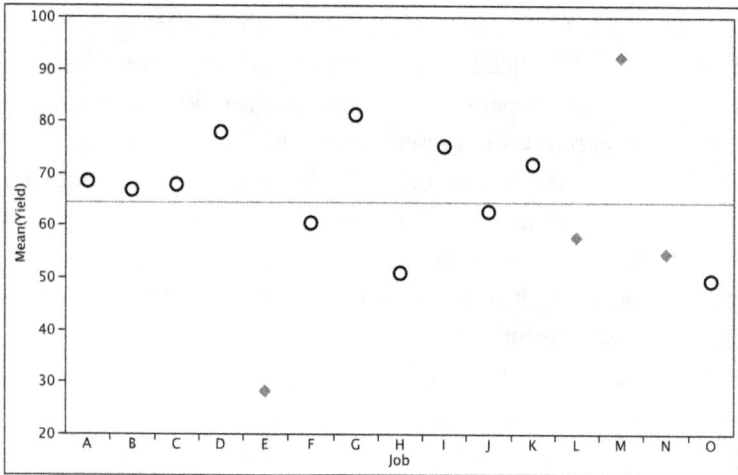

Figure 6:
Averaging buries the truth, yet this method of presentation is the one most used in business today.

This chart shows the average yield of each product type run through a factory. In this figure we use job to denote product type. The line shows the overall average yield for all of the jobs. You could make up any story you like with the data in Figure 6. You could say N is harder than job M. But is it? How much harder? What about job E? Should this company even be doing job E? Is job E's yield low because people don't know what they are doing, or is it because of the design, or is it because of the process steps?

Figure 7 is constructed using the same data! Instead of looking at the average yield for each job, we are looking at the average yield for each lot that went into each job. This is called granularity. If you don't have enough granularity in your data, you can lie. When people tell me "the data lies" the response should be, "we need more granularity." With enough granularity it is very difficult to lie.

What makes Figure 7 so powerful is the relative metric on the X-axis that was used. The X-axis is a measure of the relative difficulty of a job from 1 to 100. Engineers have learned to come up with ways to quantify things so that comparisons can be made using the combination of a number of parameters such as the length, height, shape, or roughness of a pipe or the specific gravity and viscosity of a fluid flowing through a pipe, all of which can be combined into something called a Reynolds number. This is what was done to compare the relative complexities for each job.

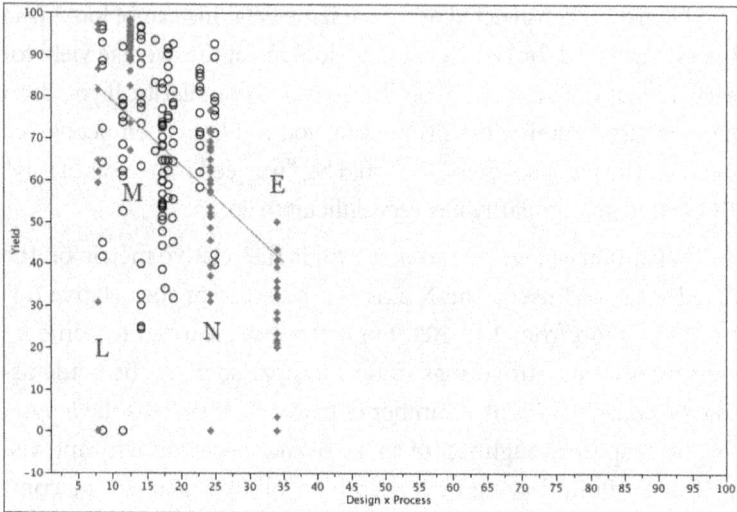

Figure 7:
The granularity in the data and the way it is organized
makes all of the previously hidden problems transparent!

There were many design features and many process features that were combined to produce a result from 1 to 100.
The most difficult product would score 100. Note that for this
company, the highest rating in production was only 35. This
was a revelation! Not only that, but the data suggests that with
a rating of 75 the predicted yield would be 0%! You would accept this job because all the parameters individually are doable.
What wasn't understood, prior to this graph, was the devastating effect of combining many of these parameters together.
You can compare this graph to the chart above. The symbols in
both charts correspond to the same jobs with the same exact
data sets. This chart is very different than the original average
data chart.

Figure 8 below focuses only on the lots for a few key jobs. Often, less is more in order to get a story.

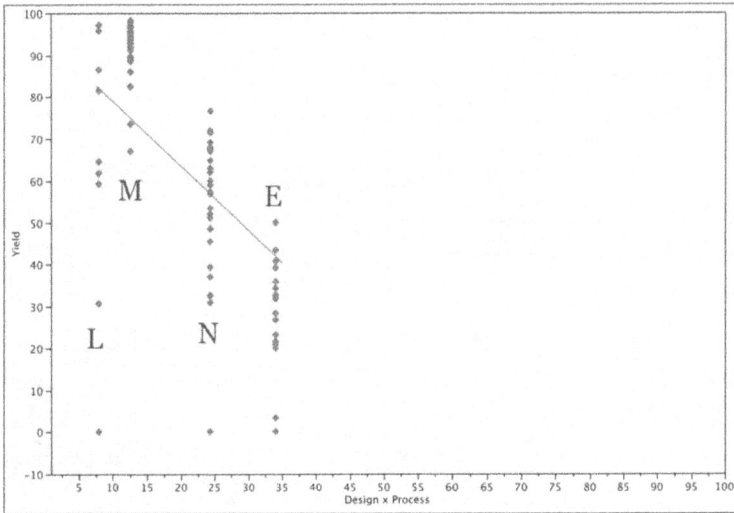

Figure 8:
It isn't the averages that are important; it is the reasons that account for the differences in variation that are important.

There are specific issues surrounding each job and when we address these issues we will make the shop better and be able to be more profitable. To get at the truth it all starts with questions. For example:

1. What accounts for the 0% lots?

2. What acounts for the large variation and eratic yield in lot L?

3. What accounts for the high average yield for job M?

4. What accounts for the low yielding lots for job M?

5. Why didn't job M have a 0% yielding lot?

6. Why is the standard deviation on lot M so much tighter than the standard deviation on lot N?

7. What parameters specifically for lot N, be it the design or in the process, accounts for the drop in yield?

8. The variation in lot N and E are very similar. Does this point to something similar about these two jobs that need to be improved?

What was found in the briefing and subsequent analysis was that some jobs required better operational technique, skill, and special handling at specific points. Reducing the spread of the yield data had a positive impact on the economics of this plant.

You will not be able to interpret Figures 7 and 8 productively if your leadership has a low level of trust and is in denial, as shown in Figures 3, 4, and 5. As a result, a company like this won't be able to get the help they need nor make the discoveries they require in order to grow their business. Instead, you will have a business that remains stagnant, where very little changes, and where it isn't fun to work. And this business will either die slowly or very quickly, depending on the market place and economic environment.

IF YOU WENT TO BUSINESS SCHOOL YOU DON'T KNOW A DAM THING!

It's a complex problem to figure out how to optimize your company such that it is competitive with any other company in the world, regardless of labor rates, marketplace, or economic environment. Too many CEOs today have an Ego DAM and a Learning DAM where they think their existing knowledge, experience, and understanding are enough. They are wrong. Now is the time to really learn how to make money in your business. Now is the time to confess that you don't know how, so you can get the help you need.

The problem for executives starts with an advanced education where they thought they were taught everything they need to know. And they have been trained in a way where they think financial analysis and cost accounting will always provide the right answer, such as, moving a factory to China, because labor is cheaper. And since the costs of handling multiple suppliers is too great, let's just buy everything from one company. Or a supply company that decided to build everything in one gigantic plant to make the most amount of money. For your company, you feel safe because you are getting your critical disk drives, for example, from the same place as your competitors. Why is that good? Because you have been trained in benchmarking—duplicate what the best companies are doing in the market place and you will make your company better.

If you aren't in business, haven't had a business education, and instead you might be a housewife, or an artist, or a musician, or a carpenter, or a professor of the liberal arts, I want to ask you something. Are there any risks to the business decisions above? Risks in doing everything just like your competitors, single sourcing from just one company, one that has everything coming from just one plant? Is it wise to put all of your supplied parts in one basket?

At the time I am writing this, Apple's stock is going down, because of the missed 2011 Q4. Everyone is talking about the iPhone sales miss. Nobody is paying attention to the real elephant in the room and what the real danger is to Apple for its next quarter—its supply of disk drives! Apple gets almost all of its disk drives from one company in Thailand.

A smart kid in elementary school can tell you there is a rainy season in Thailand called the monsoon. It typically lasts from May to October. In 2011 it really rained, and everything really flooded, including the plant that made most of the disk drives for Apple.

Tim Cook, the CEO of Apple said in *MacWorld* on October 19th, one day after Apple missed Wall Street estimates,

> *Our hearts go out to all the people in Thailand that have experienced this devastation of life and property due to the monsoon and flooding. Like many others, we source many components from Thailand and have multiple factories that supply these components. There are several factories that are not operable, and the recovery time is not known at this point. The weather hasn't really allowed an ability to assess that. From the work that we have done, our primary exposure is on the Mac. The number of drive components that are sourced in Thailand is a significant portion of our worldwide drives. I can't give you a precise accounting, but it is something I'm concerned about. I'm almost certain there will be an industry shortage; how it affects Apple I'm not sure.*

Does it stop there? No, sadly. Most business executives have been trained to think that by building the most profitable product they will make money. They have been trained to look at their business as a stagnant entity and not as an emergent, flowing stream. Companies get teams of accountants to go figure out what is the cost to make each product—cost accounting. The problem is it doesn't work.

Let's say your daughter opens up a beverage stand. You only allow her one hour to have the stand open. She can make a shake, which takes her 15 minutes, or she can just mix a pitcher or two of lemonade and always have some to pour so the customer doesn't have to wait. There are a bunch of people outside because the house right across the street is owned by a famous CEO who was just accused of cooking the books. All sorts of press and people are gathering around. The girl can make $2 on the shake or $0.50 with the lemonade. She has unlimited demand. She has unlimited capacity to make lemonade and she can serve a person every 30 seconds. She has a choice. She can make 4 shakes and make $8 or she can serve 120 people lemonade and make $60.

The right answer is obvious. If you went to business school, majored in finance, and used cost accounting you would get the wrong answer. You would tell the girl to make the shakes, because they are the most profitable! This blind spot has meant the needless departure of way too many companies and industries overseas.

Granted, most businesses are much more complex than a simple beverage stand. In all fairness, if the father was an executive he would come up with the right answer because he would clearly see the issues. But because our businesses are so complex and we have been trained in the wrong tools to solve these complex problems, we make the shakes and wonder what we are doing wrong.

Let's get back to our manager and his factory and see whether, by using modeling, we can understand his business as clearly as we can understand the girl's beverage stand.

UNDERSTAND THE FLOW OF YOUR BUSINESS! MAKE MORE LEMONADE!

In the diagram below, product moves from left to right. The round circles indicate data—such as the amount of material started, the amount of time it takes a job to go through the factory, the amount of variation that exists in the factory—that are entered into the model. Now this model will not predict a result perfectly but it will reveal what is really driving costs for many manufacturing operations. This model was created with iThink.

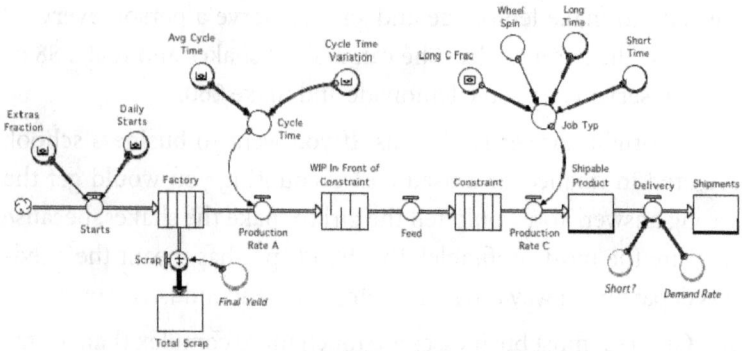

Figure 9:
Diagram for the business model used to derive the results.

Going from left to right, material to be processed enters into the operation. It can continue on or be scrapped. If it continues, it waits for the constraint (slowest operation) in the factory and then leaves to be shipped. This model shows that the unit cost is a strong function of product mix. For example, let's say your factory has a critical laser-cutting operation. It is very expensive to get more equipment. If you receive product that is very difficult to build (the shake) and mix it in with product that is easy to build (the lemonade) the number of units that can be produced per unit of time will be less. It would be like pushing your thumb on a garden hose. Since the rate at which you pay your bills doesn't change then the cost to build everything is going to be higher!

With a simple model like this you can gain insight into which product is your lemonade. But, these flow insights are just the beginning. How much material you should start, the scrap rate produced, the expected variation within certain steps, the amount of inventory on the factory floor, how well equipment is maintained, how well operators are trained, and behaviors of employees, all have huge impacts on real unit cost that will vary on a daily basis. All of them dictate the velocity at which product can travel. That is why it is never just one issue, like the price of labor. It's a multitude of issues, meaning business decisions are complex. To pretend otherwise is just a big mistake. If you aren't modeling your business and are just relying on cost accounting you might find yourself in a DAM mess.

STOP SPILLING THE LEMONADE! SHOW YOU CARE!

Remember our scatter chart with the jobs showing huge variation? This was simulated within the business model in Figure 9 and the result in Figure 10 below is for a quarter's worth of operation. The top graph shows the scrap scatter diagram, where yield is the Y-axis and level of difficulty of a part is the X-axis.

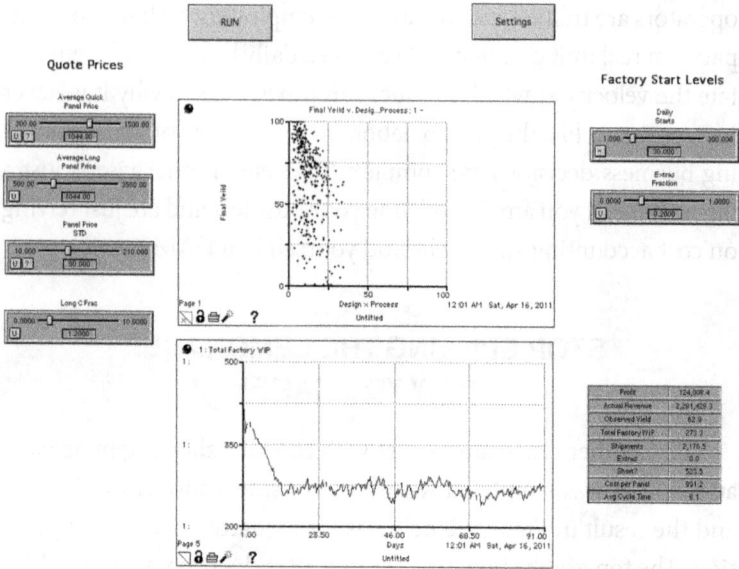

Figure 10:
The power of modeling allows you to go well beyond traditional spreadsheet analysis. This shows the current state.

When this baseline case was run for one quarter, profits were $124,008.40. Total revenue was $2,281,428.30. The average observed yield was 62.9%.

What happens when everything is kept the same, but the amount of worker related mistakes is eliminated and worker behavior is improved (they stop spilling lemonade)? This would result in a decrease in variation as shown in the top graph in Figure 11.

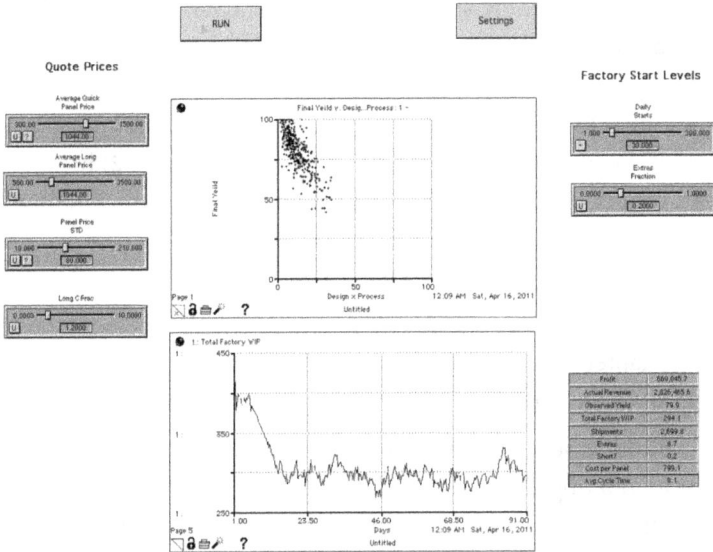

Figure 11:
By identifying the underlying truths the solution that
has the minimal cost and maximum economic benefit is
easily identified.

You now have profits of $669,045.70 on revenues of
$2,826,465.60!

In this factory, the average labor rate was $10.30 per hour.
If we plug a $1.83/hour China labor rate into our base case and
we keep the operator-related mistakes the same (the China labor
doesn't care and spill lots of lemonade) we come up with profits of
$386,280.60 with revenue of $2,306,100.50!

It isn't about labor rate. Our inability to compete is a business problem. And even after the improvements that generated $669,045.00 are
made, there is still money on the table because manufacturing, engineering, and management issues have not been touched!

This information isn't secret. There are a handful of companies in manufacturing that have very profitable businesses. They are able to compete because they know how to precisely answer the question: Do you know how to make money with your business? And if you do, you understand that 1) work is social, 2) behaviors lead results, and 3) our behaviors are governed by our thinking.

CHAPTER 12 SUMMARY

Chapter 11 is about one question: Can you admit that you need help trying to figure out how to make money in your business?

Business schools spend entirely too much time on finance and cost accounting. They spend little, if any, time on the constraints of the business. And they fail to connect the dots on how worker behaviors and the culture of the business directly affect the bottom line.

As a result, when anyone brings up data that suggests an inconvenient truth, this messenger is often shot. And when the messenger is shot, and the data revealing the truth is hidden, we see why the Ego DAM is so detrimental, because it is the source of all organizational crises. Harold Geneen was right. The worst disease that can afflict any business is egotism.

WHAT WOULD BE GOOD ABOUT LISTENING TO THE MESSENGER?

Instructions: With your PARTNER consider the questions below and try to come up with an honest answer to each. Discuss them and review all of the answers together. Start to mastermind ideas on how to make yourself a better leader of people so your company can FLOW and GROW.

By not shooting your messenger you would find...

1 = Meaningless 2 = OK 3 = Some Benefit 4 = Big Benefit 5 = Life Changing

➢ The information you gain would be?

                                               1   2   3   4   5

➢ The fact that it could prevent a major crisis, would be?

      1   2   3   4   5

➢ Discovering how you can drive true profitability of your business with a FLOW mind-set would be?

      1   2   3   4   5

➢ Pin-pointing the DAM behaviors that are holding back your company and can be changed relatively quickly would be?

      1   2   3   4   5

➢ Modeling your business and allowing the truth to emerge with a matermind would be?

      1   2   3   4   5

➢ Other messengers coming forward and not afraid of speaking the truth and caring deeply about the company would be?

      1   2   3   4   5

➢ Discovering there are a multitude of ways to make your company competitive with any other company anywhere in the world would be?

      1   2   3   4   5

➢ Knowing what data is good data, how to make data granular enough, and yet extremely easy to understand would be?

      1   2   3   4   5

➢ Your employees understanding you care and because of that they would care too would be?

                                  1   2   3   4   5

➤ Having an executive staff that is open, honest, and candid
  would be?

                              1   2   3   4   5

19 or below

Why did you even bother with this book?

20 to 39

You see a real benefit to listening to your messenger. You realize that by putting your ego on the back burner, thereby knocking
down your Ego DAM, there is less stress. The messenger wants
the business to FLOW and GROW. Instead of shooting the messenger you can now ride the wave a new era of honesty and truth.
The result will likely be a much happier work environment, that is
maximally competitive, and highly profitable.

40 or Above

There is no doubt you realize the benefit of making the hardest, and yet it is the easiest, step toward become a FLOW thinker.
When someone comes to you and tells you what is wrong with your
company, just remain quiet and listen. Ask questions, if you must.
Be open to everything the messenger shows you. There is no need
to say anything at first. Just listen and observe. Take notes. Think
about what is said. Investigate. Have others investigate. But protect
the messenger and her message. Encourage others to bring their
messages to you. And then make sound actions based on the information and explain the reasons for these actions to all in your company. You will be taking a huge step in creating a FLOW company.

EPILOGUE

The Case for Civil Disobedience

Disobedience, the rarest and most courageous of the virtues, is seldom distinguished from neglect, the laziest and commonest of vices.

—George Bernard Shaw

How highly do you rate obedience on a scale of 1 to 10, one meaning that you don't want people to be obedient and ten meaning that you want people to be obedient? Why did disobedience rate so high with someone like George Bernard Shaw?

Shaw was an activist who through his activism created change. He was a strong advocate of equal rights for men and women. Imagine living in a society where you were a second class citizen merely because you were a woman? Would obedience in that society still be a virtue?

So think again about the value of obedience. Think about how many Germans were obedient to Hitler during World War II.

Then think about Mohandas K. Gandhi, Martin Luther King Jr., Rosa Parks, Nelson Mandela, John Adams, Thomas Jefferson, and George Washington. They were all activists, were all disobedient, and all created change.

In 1849, Henry David Thoreau wrote a famous essay called *Civil Disobedience* in which he chided the government of the day, which tolerated slavery, for making obedient people agents of injustice.

When a business leader tells me he is frustrated because his work force is apathetic, I say to myself, "That is because you demand obedience from your work force. You want to come up with all of the answers. And, when you are wrong, you still want your work force to do the wrong things. If anyone opposes you, you fire them." A company full of obedient people is in DAM trouble.

Let's focus on Gandhi for a moment. Was he self-righteous? Did he have any Thinking DAMs you know of? Did he lead by force? Did he demand that the people who follow him also conform to him? The answer is no. Gandhi was a person who saw an injustice and set a standard that happened to attract a lot of people. Somehow, all of us have a solid sense in our hearts of what's just and unjust. Gandhi simply did not do what he was told by his society. He had a mind that observed and thought about the world. He had a standard of devoting his life to what was right. Gandhi had no Feelings DAM. He was devoted to his purpose—he resisted tyranny through peaceful disobedience. As a result, his life stood for something. He was heralded a great leader and is known by billions today. It is impossible to describe someone like Gandhi as self righteous.

Another form of disobedience is the natural disobedience of a child. I remember a day when my fourth grade class was marching down the hall, like an obedient army, to return our books to the library. We kept dropping our books that made an awful lot of noise as they fell. It was as if an elephant was following us. I didn't mind. But an adult would be extremely irritated. In fact our teacher, Miss Asp, lost her cool, which was rare for her. She turned around and said, "The next person who drops a book will be sent back to the classroom and not be allowed to go to the playground after the library visit!"

Well, as luck would have it, as soon as Miss Asp turned back a book slipped from my hand and dropped to the floor. Bam!

Miss Asp liked me. I was always doing things in class that were a little unusual, or saying something that would catch everyone's attention and make them laugh. It wasn't that I deliberately tried to be funny; I just spoke my mind, unfiltered. But Miss Asp was upset with me now, so I turned and obediently marched back to the classroom. As I stared out the window and watched all the other kids running out the doors to go play, Miss Asp returned. She looked at me, shook her head, and said, "Go on, be gone. Go play, Gray."

She understood that I had an independent spirit that just couldn't be tampered with.

My freshman year at St. Olaf College I was on the cross country team. The coach ordered us to remain at the school over fall break. I didn't like that idea at all. I was tired from the workouts, behind in my school work, and the dorm room was closing in on me. I wanted, in fact needed, to go home. So I decided to go home. I didn't care if coach threw me off the team. At the time, the team mattered less than my desire to go home. When I returned after the four day weekend, coach pulled me aside and started to lecture me, then stopped mid-sentence, paused and took a completely different tone. As though we were equals sitting on the same side of the table, he said, "I am not getting through to you am I?"

I didn't say a word.

"I see," he said. "Go join the rest of the team."

Unexpectedly, we won the Minnesota Intercollegiate Athletic Conference cross country championship that year. My best time that season was 26:25 for the five-mile race, a time at the start of the season I didn't think was possible for me. Coach got more out of me than anyone ever had before. And he got a tremendous amount from everyone on the team. He had built up an enormous amount of trust, but also raised each of our standards. He knew how to manage a very diverse group of young men and not kill their spirit. The entire team loved him for what he did for us. I loved him because he recognized my need to be me.

When you are the one disobedient fish in an ocean of obedience, you stand alone. As a new hire at AlliedSignal, I challenged Mark Bulriss, president of the division where I had been placed. I believed a corporate initiative was putting the customer last. I felt the initiative was wrong and I said so. Others agreed, but they remained obediently silent. I stood alone, the perfect target. I was in trouble.

Management applied a huge amount of pressure to try to make me go along with their rules. I wouldn't. It wasn't until a year later, when the initiative was changed and the customer was put first, that all of the pressure was relieved. It taught me that there is a significant price you must pay if you choose to be disobedient.

At another company I saw visuals that showed exactly how the plant was doing, the good and the bad. The manager didn't want to hide anything and the employees didn't want anything hidden. Everything—plant cleanliness, throughput, process control, and more—was posted on the walls and updated continually. Supervisors and operators conducted meetings in front of these charts. Everyone in the plant liked seeing the information because they wanted to be engaged in what was going on.

When the company CEO saw this, he didn't like it and ordered the material taken down. He only wanted information on the walls that showed the shop was performing perfectly. He was afraid that anything that showed a problem would be perceived negatively by customers who came through the facility. This meant valuable information would be hidden and the stories of what was really happening would be lost. After talking to me, the plant manager decided to disobey and keep the information posted on the walls.

This was a tough situation. The CEO expected complete obedience. The manager was trying to create a new, transparent, trusting, and collaborative culture at the plant. There were good reasons why he needed the good and the bad shown visually.

The CEO was in jeopardy of losing an outstanding leader because of the value he placed on having subordinates obey him. His focus on obedience could have led to the weakening of the company.

What happens when two people severely disagree on an issue, unable to budge an inch because both believe they are right? Here's a story that will help put this into perspective:

I have gone down the Grand Canyon on a raft several times. Each time I have gone down there with a group of people a great conflict emerges around the big questions: Is there a God? Does my life have meaning?

There is a reason why this happens. At many places you see limestone cliffs rising thousands of feet into the air. These cliffs represent the slow process of marine life dying, falling to the bottom of an ancient sea bed, and being compacted. This process spans billions of years and was occurring well before the time of the dinosaurs. In fact, the relatively thin band of rock near the top of the canyon demonstrates how recent dinosaurs arrived and how relatively short they lived.

As you look up from the bottom of the canyon, viewing cliff after cliff, you begin to appreciate how long life existed before dinosaurs even showed up and where we show up is almost un-detectable. The simple reality is we are irrelevant to planet Earth, past, present, and future.

Later in the day, around a campfire, you look up at the vast Milky Way—our galaxy—in which Earth is a mere speck. Three quarters of a century ago, the astronomer Edwin Hubble looked at the Milky Way. Using the Hooker Telescope, which was the big-gest of its day, Hubble focused in on these mysterious things called Nebula. What he proved was Nebula were other distant galaxies. The universe was not the Milky Way! In fact what we know today there are actually billions upon billions of other galaxies like ours in the universe. The simple reality is Earth is insignificant to the universe, past, present, and future.

With almost every Grand Canyon rafting trip that my friend Paul Knauth puts on for Arizona State University's School of Earth & Space Exploration, a crisis emerges out of this humbling reality. This crisis becomes the source of the conflict and inevitable debate around the big questions.

One night around the campfire it happened as if on que. Two friends of mine engaged in a heated debate. One had deep religious convictions. The other was very scientific. The religious friend was an ex-Army colonel who fought bravely in Vietnam. The scientific friend was a distinguished professor.

As the debate began, the professor's position was, in essence, "The Earth is billions of years old; religion is false; science is right."

As you would expect from an Army man, the colonel aggres-sively engaged in the rebuttal, "You mean to tell me this was all random chance? That all of this happened as an accident!"

As I sat there and watched, it went back and forth, getting more and more heated.

Later at dinner, I approached the professor and explained to him why what he was telling my friend the Colonel was so upsetting. I related some of the stories the Colonel had told me about Vietnam, how he had seen and survived Hell, and nobody was ever going to tell him it was for nothing.

The professor suddenly understood, and then listened to the Colonel and asked about his stories. He began to see the Colonel for the fine man that he was. In turn, the Colonel began to see the professor as a provocative friend. Their differences on how they both interpreted what they saw wasn't important. What was important was how to help each other deal with their insignificance that was so obvious being in the canyon; an insignificance they both rejected! This was the common enemy that bonded them together like two brothers.

With the big questions, it isn't about determining who is right or wrong. It is about whether we want to obey the facts all around us that scream, "You are insignificant!" Only a healthy ego could believe it is significant in the face of so much evidence to the contrary, and it is a battle people have fought since the beginning of humanity.

It is also the reason why ego is a good thing. Without our ego we would be instantly crushed. Without our ego, we could not stand up and, in an act of supreme disobedience, declare to the entire infinite universe, "I am significant!"

Why was I reading *The Brothers Karamazov* the day the businessman walked into my dorm room with his wife and daughter? Why did I point out my attraction to the study of history and philosophy to him? I was doing what I felt my mind needed to learn. I was following my own path that was helping me become me. I was allowed to pursue any course of study, where my dad felt obligated to follow the wishes and be obedient to his father. Nobody had the right to judge what I liked to study and what I felt I needed to be me. That is why my respect for this businessman that entered my dorm room was reduced to the size of a pencil head when he intimated I was wasting my time and I should be developing practical skills.

At those moments I deeply appreciated the lessons my father taught me. Even though he didn't like my disobedience, he knew it was necessary. My dad knew the greatest gift a father could give his son was how to be a man with the courage to stand up for what he believes, for the beliefs that come directly from his heart. When I asked him in his weakened state, what would his advice be for me for the rest of my life, he said simply, "Always be true to who you are and keep an open mind."

His simple words may not mean much to you, but these simple words continue to have a profound impact on my life. You need to know more about my father to understand.

On occasion my sister would tell my father, "Well you aren't perfect either." And my dad would reply, "No but I am very close."

My dad was attracted to highly intelligent, flawed, creative people. They were from all sorts of backgrounds and professions. My dad's parties were a great gathering of these friends who I remember as bohemians: believers in unconventional lifestyles and thinking involving musical, artistic, and literary pursuits. For someone that was so disciplined in his profession and at times had to demand absolute obedience from his staff, he surrounded himself with people who lived disobedient lives. People free to pursue life, liberty, and pursuit of happiness with all of the drama, comedy, and tragedy it entailed. In this environment with his friends my dad felt most free.

At work it was a completely different story. When we need a surgeon to save our life the last thing we want to hear is, "I am not sure and I don't know." We want someone that is righteously confident in what they are doing and we want to be completely obedient to him or her in the hope that we will not die. This may be less true today, but it was absolutely true in the late 1950's and early 1960's, which was when my father was trained.

Seeing this as a necessary behavior when the situation was critical and life threatening, it was natural for my father to be that same righteous way towards me and my life decisions. So we would fight. I would be disobedient. And I would accuse him of having a closed mind. I didn't understand what was really going on. I often failed to see, once we moved past the fight, how he would support me in my own disobedient vision and respect me for being true to myself like his bohemian friends.

But I judged him harshly. I expected him to be perfect in everything. And when I learned how sick he was, he knew, even though I didn't show it, I was angry at him. He could have lived a healthier lifestyle. He could have seen his doctor regularly. He could have asked for help a long time ago. He was about to die and it was his fault. I felt righteously entitled. And he felt guilty.

My dad knew at a time like this it was important for a father and son to reconcile. So instead of answering the question, "What advice do you have for me for the rest of my life" knowing full well I wouldn't listen to it anyway, he answered the question of how I could reconcile my relationship with him.

In order to understand my dad's answer let's look at one of the most enigmatic personalities of American history, Thomas Jefferson. He wrote these important words when writing one of the most disobedient documents of all time, the Declaration of Independence.

We hold these truths to be self-evident, that all men are created equal, that they are endowed by their Creator with certain unalienable Rights, that among these are Life, Liberty, and the pursuit of Happiness.

Jefferson was a slave owner! It wasn't one or two slaves to tend a small farm. It was a large plantation totaling thousands of acres where over his lifetime he owned hundreds of slaves. Jefferson only freed two slaves when he was alive. With each opportunity to free slaves Jefferson wouldn't do it. For example, a close friend willed his estate to Jefferson on the condition and mutual understanding that Jefferson's slaves would go free. When his friend died, Jefferson went back on his word, kept his slaves, and kept the money for himself!

Jefferson lived extravagantly and in many ways like a king. For example he spent large sums of money buying extremely expensive wines, building up an enormous collection, which you can see remnants of when you visit his home in Monticello. The shipping costs from Europe alone were enough to buy many slaves their freedom. After he died, his remaining 130 slaves had to be sold to pay his debts!

Jefferson was incredibly selfish. His actions went absolutely against the truth he wrote in our Declaration of Independence. How can we reconcile that the same person who wrote "Life, Liberty, and the pursuit of Happiness" also treated hundreds of people so abominably?

There are only a few places to look on how to do this and one of those places is the Bible. During the time of Jesus, leaders of the powerful Jewish religious sect called the Pharisees wanted to test Jesus's understanding of their law. They asked him this very simple question, "What was the greatest commandment in the Law?" and Jesus states {Matthew 22:36–40}.

Love the Lord your God with all your heart and with all your soul and with all your mind.

And he continues...

Love your neighbor as yourself.

Jefferson knew his life had strayed far from the truth he wrote in the Declaration of Independence. He wrote...

Every human being must be viewed according to what it is good for. For not one of us, no, not one, is perfect. And were we to love none who had imperfection, this world would be a desert for our love.

Understanding my father's words I came to love and appreciate him more with all of his flaws and contradictions. I was disobedient to him many times. But with what he told me I have found myself not only obedient, but bound to my father and his words...

Be true to yourself. Keep an open mind.

"Be true to yourself," is having the courage to be who we really are. It demands moments of disobedience. "Keep an open mind," is a way of fully accepting others, flaws and all, and at moments requires obedience. Figuring out the harmony between these two ideas—being disobedient and true to ourselves and being obedient and true to others—is what life is all about. And when we can do that we become the best person we can be. Only then do we stand a chance of building a great company free of DAM problems.

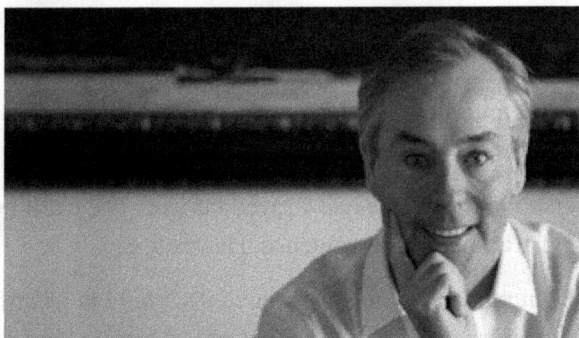

ABOUT GRAY MCQUARRIE

Gray McQuarrie is founder and president of Grayrock & Associates, LLC and founder of the Flow Thinkers Group.

Gray is the primary inventor for the patent Compensation Model and Registration Simulation Apparatus and Method for Manufacturing Printed Circuit Boards, which increased productivity between suppliers and fabricators in this global industry on an exponential scale. He has worked for and consulted with small companies as well as Fortune 100 companies. A six sigma black belt, a product development master, and winner of the premier achievement award for customer satisfaction given out by Larry Bossidy, CEO of AlliedSignal, Gray is passionate about developing systems that can be implemented quickly. He has a liberal arts education from St. Olaf College, where he received a B.A., and a professional education from the University of Minnesota, where he earned a degree in Chemical Engineering.

Gray is one of the few consultants who has to practice what he preaches every day, and this book is a reflection of that practical step-by-step approach to solving some of today's toughest business issues.

You can learn more about Gray and Grayrock & Associates, LLC at businessagilitysolutions.com.